STRANGERS DOING
ALZHEIMER'S

A True Story

STRANGERS DOING ALZHEIMER'S

THE ASSAULT ON CAREGIVERS

J.P. RIPPLE

STRANGERS DOING ALZHEIMER'S
THE ASSAULT ON CAREGIVERS

iUniverse books may be ordered through booksellers or by contacting:

iUniverse
1663 Liberty Drive
Bloomington, IN 47403
www.iuniverse.com
1-800-Authors (1-800-288-4677)

Because of the dynamic nature of the Internet, any web addresses or links contained in this book may have changed since publication and may no longer be valid. The views expressed in this work are solely those of the author and do not necessarily reflect the views of the publisher, and the publisher hereby disclaims any responsibility for them.

Any people depicted in stock imagery provided by Thinkstock are models, and such images are being used for illustrative purposes only. Certain stock imagery © Thinkstock.

ISBN: 978-1-4917-8345-0 (sc)
ISBN: 978-1-4917-8944-5 (e)

Library of Congress Control Number: 2016902469

Print information available on the last page.

iUniverse rev. date: 02/19/2016

CONTENTS

CH. 1 INTRODUCTION

I was caregiver for my eighty-five-year-old mother almost four years. In late-winter, I found mom walking to a neighbor's yard in below-freezing temperatures. Her primary-care physician was notified about her wandering at 3 a.m. in the snow wearing only a cotton robe. I ask her doctor for permission to take her to a Behavioral Hospital for an evaluation. She had been hallucinating and delusional for almost a week. He made an appointment for the following day. My next-door neighbor helped take mom to the hospital; Alice said I would need her help and volunteered. Alice was right, mom objected to a two-day stay and being away from her dogs. Two days couldn't be spared in her busy schedule she reminded the nurses and staff. Mom added, "J.P. can't feed and care for Sarah and Daisy like she could during those two days!" She reminded staff. "Two days without me will be a disaster for Sarah and Daisy. Sadly she said, "What will ever become of them?"

The primary-care doctor should be a caregiver's workhorse. They are going to do the "heavy lifting" for caregivers. If they don't, ask your insurance for a list of physicians with experience in senior care. It is easy to switch p-c doctors when the need arises.

Mom reassured me there wasn't anything wrong with her memory. "Memory loss was normal for her age," she said. Her primary-care physician promised her stay wouldn't be more than two days. I knew that was a lie because an evaluation at the prestige hospital covers diet, monitoring medications, observing behavior, and a battery of mental tests.

Mom's doctor was working for me by making it easy for her to say, "Yes!" My guess the stay would be at least seven days and that's what I told friends and relatives. Her doctor's stratagem did the job and two days seemed manageable to mom. And, with a little persuasion from Alice, mom endorsed her doctor's suggestion for an evaluation.

She would be placed into a group setting and we were excited about professionals observing her reaction with others. She had been a recluse since dad passed away over twenty years ago. We thought she would have to be placed into an assisted-living home if her diagnosis was Stage 5 or 6 Alzheimer's. However, there was one big problem: Could she live in such a place and get along with others her age? That question was one of many we wanted answered before her stay ended. Mom's dad died from complications of Alzheimer's. Mom's mother had early-stage Alzheimer's in her seventies. The prognosis for mother wasn't looking good with so many close-family members with dementia.

Everything sounded great and we were all on board for the experiment. Mom would be living in a ten-patient ward for two days. There would be comprehensive testing followed by a psychiatric evaluation. Our primary goal was to monitored her behavior because we had been looking at nursing homes about thirty miles away. TIP: Some people can't or won't work with staff or patients in a ward. If your loved one is stubborn, ask the Intake Nurse for suggestions before admitting your loved one.

After eight days, mom seemed restless and I could see aggression building. I visited daily between 7-8:30 p.m. and could see a change in attitude. Mom was becoming anxious and agitated. The hospital stay was taking its toll and each day was a struggle. I notified the social worker about her difficulties. The social worker was blunt, "Your mother is having a difficult time adjusting to our routine. Your mother has stopped working with us and is resisting our methods." The social worker agreed with the psychiatrist, mom's questions didn't have anything to do with her care: Why do we have a long lunch and a short breakfast?, Why does the doctor ignore me and visit someone else?, Why are the patients fighting staff?, and my memory is fine so why don't you let me go home?

I couldn't understand the reason for the aggressive symptoms because she had been taking anxiety and depression medication before admission. After visiting with her nurse, mom wasn't working well with staff and for some reason had a grudge against the psychiatrist. On my first visit, mother mentioned the doctor was evading her questions. She was questioning the clinic's "plan-of-treatment" at that first visit. I walked to her doctor's office next to the hospital to asked the doctor why he scheduled her for another two weeks. He wasn't in his office, but wrote a letter describing her behavior during hospitalization so I could obtain guardianship.

After that letter, a social worker phoned all pertinent information about mom's treatment. We met daily at 2 p.m. to discuss treatments. The psychiatrist thought she couldn't understand any medical condition or cared about their efforts. The psychiatrist relayed all information to the social worker and counselors. Staff thought mom wasn't serious about her health and didn't know why she was admitted over a week ago. The way the staff explained things to me, they thought she could harm herself by wandering as soon as she was released!

I was shocked to hear their prognosis and asked why they thought she was in danger. The nurse read a memo from mom's "plan" sheet that mentioned: Ms. Dollie's interview on Wednesday threatened the staff that she would wander, if she wanted to, when released. Her statement led me to believe she might have a psychosis.

This statement seemed to have halted all treatment. The memo, now in hospital records, appalled me and I didn't know how to respond. Why would she threaten staff and force the clinic to curtail all treatment? What stage of Alzheimer's was mom reflecting in her present behavior?

I asked the nurse at the main desk if patients made phone calls throughout the day. My hypothesis concerned mom being prompted to say and do things and I wanted it stopped! This wasn't going to be a two-week vacation. The nurse replied, "Patients aren't allowed to make calls, but they can receive and make calls during visiting hours." However, after visiting with her primary nurse and social worker, my impression was a troublesome patient and a staff that hadn't decided what to do—they were taking their time.

The social workers thought mom could harm herself wandering and would have to return for further treatment. We were perplexed by the new information and didn't know what to do about the predicament.

Should we take her home or ask them to keep her another two weeks? Mom was frustrated about all the frivolous interviews and treatment. I made the decision to let her go home and see how things turn out! It was a big mistake and I took responsibility for my actions! She should have spent another two to eight weeks at this juncture. We should have known the Behavioral Hospital had a better handle on her condition and agreed with them she wasn't ready to go home. Doctors thought mom was still in Stage 2 or 3 Alzheimer's and would report those stages for many months.

The clinic hesitated to release mom after eight days. They reminded me being released generated strict guidelines for behavior. A social worker read the rules and had mother to initial each one. I almost laughed at their efforts—mom wasn't the kind of person to follow rules—they should know that by now! Mom did things her way and if it hurts someone's feelings, especially family, she didn't care! I mentioned to her doctor that mom fought family, but was always polite to people outside the family. They thought is was either a "control issue" or came from family tribulation. I believe her doctors modified their views about a "control issue" before the final evaluation. I remember mom telling staff both husbands had a control issued with her. However, a social worker thought the opposite was true.

As mom walked to her room to pack her things, I noticed a handful of patients huddled around a table near the exit. I heard them discussing mom's situation. Once they knew for sure mom was leaving the ward, they chanted loud enough for everyone to hear, "Ms Dollie will be back, Ms Dollie will be back, She'll be back, Ms. Dollie will be back!" The chanting was so loud mom could hear it from her room. She walked to the middle of the hallway and replied, "No, I'm not coming back!, I'm not coming back!, Just wait and see! I am not coming back!" A woman, looked to be in her seventies, got the final word: "She'll be back, you can count on that!"

Mom had serious problems adjusting to the hospital, staff, and patients in her ward. However, she did make a few friends and introduced me to them. We were all wondering if she could live in a nursing home or an assisted- living unit after failing the experiment. I thought the answer was definitely, "Don't even try!"

My step-dad and I fished together for years before he succumb to leukemia.On one of our fishing trips, he made an odd statement, "I hate dying because of your mother!" I ask him what he meant and he said, "She can't make it on her own without me!" I think he knew she had dementia and possibly psychosis when he made that statement! I reminded him our family isn't small! We'll find a family member who will take good care of her, if I can't! Dad said, "I want you to know that I want her to live in our house until her death. I think she will be okay if you are involved with her care." I added, "My Army experience was a good education.

The hospital staff moved mom's room assignment twice to make her more comfortable and adjust to the ward. Staff had to remind her to clear her table several times. She wasn't allowed to take naps and it just killed her! However, she never questioned my reason for asking her p-c doctor to admit her. Her problems were unique and the hospital hesitated releasing her on schedule. Furthermore, the psychiatrist was a brilliant man. He reminded me, "Your mother never really understood why she was admitted!" Mom complained about the staff and how badly she was treated. Her stories seemed contrived and detestable towards her psychiatrist. Staff ignored her request for another room, a longer lunch break, and medication for a nagging-sinus problem. We understood it was dementia running the "show." I took notes, but said nothing to staff or relatives about the atrocious behavior the hospital staff had to endure those eight days.

I heard a strange story as I helped pack her clothes. She told about a black woman coming into her room at night and stealing her makeup. Mom repeated the story about the woman to her roommate. She replied, "We never saw the woman again after my roommate reported her to the desk!" I'm not a psychologist, but she had to be experiencing some kind of paranoid behavior related to dementia. I tried to ignore the stealing remarks about the African-American woman because we were about to go home. I didn't want any problems during dismissal after hearing that story.

Also, I expected a long-complex diagnosis from the doctors and staff. Later, they informed me it was a form of delusional behavior. TIP: When caregivers hear the word "suspicion," fear should run through your body, followed by a cold sweat. A lot of grief and possibly legal action could be headed your way. I would soon get a taste of its proclivity for caregivers followed by an appearance in court.

I visited everyday and could see my mother's dementia-related "suspicion" getting worse. As her son and caregiver, they bombarded me with Alzheimer's information and requests for more treatment. They requested ten more days but I turned them down. I noticed an "assault on caregivers" about that time. Everyone questioned me about having Power or Guardianship before answering any further questions about mom's care or treatment. A social worker offered to contact an attorney for "Power" or Guardianship help. They must know something I don't we often wondered! A longtime-family attorney said he had no clue as to what was going on with her care. However, the attorney ask for $1,500 to initiate Guardianship!

Staff worried that mom could harm herself if they agreed to an early dismissal. By that time, we were tired; however, we agreed to let her go home but odd behavior had to monitored and recorded. The staff gave me a long list of phone numbers to report any wandering behavior in the next ten days. Any wandering was to be reported as soon as it occurred to the social worker. They reminded me they were there 24/7 to help make mom's live safer! They insisted she could harm herself and should be monitored during this time.

Mom's wanderings, all at night, didn't slow down after being released. She had one wandering-by-foot and two wanderings-by-ambulance in the following eight days. The Behavioral Hospital was correct releasing mom too soon. The week following dismissal, she violated her safety agreement five times. During that first week, she invented a new way of wandering: wandering-by-ambulance! It was an incredible thing to witness an elderly woman manipulating so many professionals. We didn't know if someone told her how to summons an ambulance or she discovered it on her own. The latter was most likely the case. The wandering-by- ambulance was likely accidental after spilling coffee on the kitchen floor.

During mom's last birthday party, we had lots of cake and coffee. She was having the time of her life—we actually saw her smile.

She hadn't been that happy in a long time. After spilling coffee on on the kitchen floor, she bent over to clean the coffee and accidentally squeezed the LifeBand button on her necklace. Immediately, she discovered the button had lots of power. A loud voice suddenly shook the room: "Ms. Dollie this is Susan, do you need help?"

As soon as the voice asked the question, mom said, "No, I accidentally push the button!" "So you don't need any help at this time?" Susan asked again. Mom replied, "No!"

Finally, mom could get away from the fat man looking into her windows at night by pushing a button. Pushing this button gathered people who would visit and sympathize about those dangerous teenagers in her front yard. Pushing this button summoned the sheriff and ambulance in a hurry. It turned out to be a "miracle" button!

Once she got to one of the five hospitals in the area, mom would say or do anything to be admitted. The staff got a taste of what paranoia behavior was like for an elderly woman. Her drama was the same at every hospital: "I AM IN DANGER IN MY HOME, YOU ARE NOT GOING TO HURT ME, ARE YOU?" Mom repeated these statements over and over until doctors told her to stop! Her drama never worked because the supplemental insurance refused to hospitalize a patient that has no diagnosed-physical problem. The ER staff spent hours laughing at her attempt to persuade them to admit her; however, the staff incessantly stared at me.

We were amazed how mom's mind could scheme early in the disease. She never could talk her way into a hospital. However, She did hit the jackpot on a Thursday night at the Heart Hospital. The new hospital didn't have her records and instead of calling her mental-health hospital or her caregiver, they called the sheriff in the next county. WHAT COULD GO WRONG?

She told the ER staff, "I am a sick woman with a possible stroke, and I'm very dizzy!" Most doctors laughed at the textbook-version of a dementia- related quandary. Time after time, doctors gave nausea pills for dizziness and sent her on her way. Mom couldn't understand why she was going home so soon. All four MRI's, from four different hospitals, came back clear and proved there was a lot of "faking" strokes on her agenda. When you don't share medical records, four MRI's add up to a lot of time and money! Are you listening supplemental-health insurers and hospitals that don't share health records? If this hospital had mom's records, they would have done the right thing and sent her back to her Behavioral Hospital for four to six weeks of treatment.

That isn't what mom wanted to hear. She wanted to hear: We are going to admit you for a day or two for observations!" She heard those magic words two years ago after a bout with food poisoning. Mom vomited for three days and took only liquids. She was a happy camper during the stay! She talked to friends and relatives for weeks about how painful it was those three days. She soaked the empathy from those who called during and after the hospitalization.

I thought it was some sort of cruel joke until deputies ask me to sign the summons. One of the two officers helped find mom on two occasions. I thought he was too involved in the case and e-mailed him questioning his integrity. The officer ignored both e-mails and his action gave me some concern. I visited with his boss and he and I disagreed on everything we discussed. Police training needs a lot of work in my opinion. Four months later, we filed formal complaints against the officer for abusing an Alzheimer's patient. Not taking her to her Behavioral Hospital as directed by her Adult-Safety Agreement was a critical mistake by this officer and hospital staff. He took the wrong approach when he took her to ADULT CARE, INC.—a safe house in a nearby town. His actions caused many problems including my bills of over $1,200. TIP: Try not to react if your loved one blames you for something. Don't argue with the person.

Explain to others that the person is acting this way because he/she has early- stage Alzheimer's disease. Caregivers are often accused of false acts but it is the disease talking and not your loved one. Act professional around people and educate them about the disease. Most people are illiterate about Alzheimer's and have heard or seen later stages— when patients have serious problems and need constant supervision. Alzheimer's patients can wander at any stage of the disease and that is why caregivers need to be vigilant. The stress can weigh heavily on caregivers and family, but dad/mom can live many years at home if you can control the wandering.

Alzheimer's gets worse over time. Although symptoms can vary widely, the first problem many people notice is forgetfulness severe enough to affect their ability to function at home or at work, or to enjoy lifelong hobbies.[1]

Caregivers are usually the first to notice changes in their loved ones and are the experts. Doctors may want to review your observations in a well organized notebook. Please keep track of any changes in behavior in a pocket notebook or journal with month and day of the week at the top of each page. Remember, you are not alone caring for your loved one!

CH. 2 ALZHEIMER'S AND OUR MEDICAL SYSTEM

Memory loss and confusion may cause a person with Alzheimer's to perceive things in new and unusual ways. Individuals may become suspicious of those around them, even accusing others of theft, infidelity, or other improper behavior. Sometimes a person may misinterpret what he or she sees and hears.[2]

Finally, we knew mom was very sick from the "clinical evaluation" and her doctor's final diagnosis: "Dementia with Lewy bodies. We have evidence that mom's mother, dad, and a few relatives most likely the same dementia in their mid-sixties. Mom's dad had the dementia that led to Alzheimer's disease. Grandpa always reported to me that he was often dizzy at work. I am not a doctor, but I believe grandpa had symptoms of both Alzheimer's dementia and dementia with Lewy bodies.

Experts estimate that a skilled physician can diagnose Alzheimer's with more than 90 percent accuracy. Physicians can almost always determine that a person has dementia, but it may sometimes be difficult to determine the exact cause. [3]

A pocket notebook was always with me when visiting mom. Any changes were recorded immediately in the notebook during the eight days. I witnessed new and strange behavior, and kept track of everything mentioned to turn over to her Intake Coordinator for review. Mom would tell stories about various people in the unit next to hers. The unit was only visible through the cafeteria windows. She called them "crazy" because they would physically attack staff members. She witnessed physical attacks on a daily basis and called them "terrible incidents." She insinuated sexual abuse was going on in that ward among staff and patients. The doctors were looking into the possibility of mom having "dementia and psychosis" at the same time. I was told they couldn't find evidence of psychosis in mother.

I believe her strange observations were all hallucinations caused by the weird behavior of roommates during her treatment. She was among strangers that had a host of mental problems. As you could imagine, our family was glad to see the eight-day evaluation come to an end.

Caregivers requesting evaluations should compare notes of any new behavior they witness. This notebook should be shared with the p-c doctor, intake nurses, and relatives. Likewise, any shocking statements should be recorded with date and time. Finally, the p-c doctor wanted to see her within a week for any strange behavior and wanderings. The behavioral clinic made the p-c doctor responsible for relaying events to them as soon as they occurred.

Mother began wandering-by-ambulance when she would get bored and wanted some action. ER doctors never approached me about twice-a-week trips. She could "get away" from locked doors and visit people who were always attentive and friendly: "Hi Ms. Dollie, it is good to see you again." How is your health after that last visit?" I laughed at all the personal activity that was just for "show!" However, my friends weren't so happy about ER behavior that they thought promoted wandering! They wanted to discuss the matter with the hospital CEO, but I thought is was a waste of time and could cause problems. We preferred an ER that got down to business and warned about the dangers of wandering.

We liked mom's p-c doctor because he was young and didn't have a busy practice. We could see him the following day for a wandering event or an ER visit. Don't let neighbors or relatives tell you to let your loved one visit the doctor alone. Our neighbor told me not to say anything about mom's behavior to the doctor. Alice thought I was influencing the doctor for more medication. She said, "It would be best if you wouldn't visit the doctor at all; let your mother visit on her own." It was upsetting to me, so my reply was firm: "Alice, we know you want to help my mother, but we have to do as the doctor says. We know for a fact that mom tries to manipulates nurses and doctors. We have seen her manipulate doctors and nurses on the last three ER trips. I am her caregiver, so please don't worry. Most doctors are intelligent and experienced to do the right thing. Let's give them a chance to do their job." TIP: Be firm with your friends and relatives that arouse such stupidity. A "take charge" attitude is sometimes a necessary trait for caregivers.

If you aren't satisfied, ask your supplemental insurance for a new doctor. I asked for a new doctor for mom and one for myself. My doctor wouldn't schedule a physical for me. I was 50 at the time and never had a physical. The insurance company agreed with me and sent a list of doctors practicing in my area. Some doctors hate their practice because they can't type. Ask any doctor, what is the worst part of your job: Paperwork and not being able to type. A "sour puss" will often turn offensive and complain about the medical field. My question: "Dr., if you have practiced for 30-years,why haven't you taken a course on how to type? You could have invented a machine that does "short hand for medical records by now!" Caregivers should consider a new doctor to replace "sour pusses." It is your civic duty to complain about the men and women who shouldn't be practicing medicine. TIP: Don't fall in love with your doctor! Caregivers must avoid some of them at all costs because we have enough problems. One of my big mistakes was not getting an older doctor for mom. Good doctors need years of experience in Alzheimer's treatment and care. I blame her young doctor for many of my problems as a caregiver.

A foot specialist moved into our area and had poor bedside manners and possibly psychological problems. He would always make negative comments about ObamaCare. His comments would throw cold water on the health-care plan. He made it a point to mention the program as often as he could during office visits. I decided it would be best mom not use him and avoid his immature-bedside manners. The insurance company asked the reason for changing: I told them he had poor-bedside manners! Caregivers must be ready and willing to change doctors if they stop working for you or have pitiful bedside manners. Caregivers know it isn't a big deal and it doesn't take a lot of time to change doctors. You are not alone! People get mad at doctors all the time! TIP: Caregivers should pay close attention to beside manners. I know many caregivers look for this personality trait on the first visit. If the doctor lacks interest in grandma or doesn't answer your questions in simple language it's time to move on!

In my opinion, some of the best doctors are GP's (General Practice). They are generally in their late forties or fifties and they "KNOW THEIR STUFF!" I have talked about young doctors in this book, but I would personally not select one for myself. My doctor must have at least twenty years experience and in his/her forties or fifties.

Caregivers walk on quicksand most of the time working with the elderly!States are imposing new guidelines and evaluations for caregivers every year. My attorney says he worries that the future looks bleak for caregivers. Caregivers are increasingly hiring help from a pool of caregivers in the community. As I have said, we need all the help we can find to do a good job. Therefore, caregivers will be hiring caregivers in the foreseeable future. Check with your attorney for new laws and guidelines in the field.

Mom's discharge medications were changed to four and to be continued until further notice: Duloxetine 60 mg for major depressive disorder, Famotidine 10 mg for gastric reflux, Levothyroxine 75 mcg for thyroid, mirtazapine 7.5 mg for antidepression, and Travataz Z 0.0004 % ophthalmic solution for wide-angle glaucoma. Famotidine is an over the counter drug to be used as needed.

For some reason, mom would go through periods or "cycles" of "suspicion" behavior after leaving the Behavioral Hospital. She would be "On" for a day then 'Off' for a day. This "Off" and "On" predicted the mood for the day. Her mood was often very bad in the "Off" stage. Thoughts of the woman stealing her makeup provoked mom for days. If she or I brought up the theft, it would assure she drifted to "Off." This woman could make her drift to "Off" most of the time; however, anxiety medication moved her back to "On." We were so excited about the response to the medication— it turned her "On" most of the time. The anxiety drugs made her easy to talk to about things that concerned us. Her mood and mental clarity were agreeable when she was on anxiety medication. She would always say yes to traveling with her dogs when her mood was pleasant.

We didn't think much about the complaint of theft in her room, but some worried that it was such a traumatic event she might not recover. We had a good reason to think that: Mom would explain what happened in vivid details and fear gripped her face days after the she left the hospital. This fear worried me that it wouldn't let go and she would need depression medication. I knew it was likely paranoia—a type of delusional behavior of false beliefs—that a person thinks are real. I am guessing she developed the paranoia because she was around so many strangers in the ward. It was easy to understand how she got "anxiety" from a stranger stealing things out of her room! Also, most caregivers agreed with me that the event would likely cause more problems for mom if she participated in some form of "therapy."

We thought about the fear and helplessness she was experiencing and how to remove the fear for a day or two. Her eyes begged me to take her from the Behavioral Hospital. TIP: If you admit your loved one and they soon develop "suspicion" behavior, tell the Intake Nurse immediately. That interview will determine if you can make further arrangements with the consent of the hospital. The fear seemed real, but could it jeopardize her stay if I antagonized the hospital staff. We never mentioned the theft again even to friends and relatives. I prayed the problem wouldn't cause more delusions or hallucinations.

An auto mechanic lived next door and serviced mom's car. He thought he was the best mechanic in town. On one occasion, he just couldn't repair her aging car. He gave up and proclaimed, "Sometimes mechanical problems have a way of working themselves out! I never told him I didn't have his philosophy repairing cars. TIP: Don't' wait for the car to break down or your loved one to get well on his own! Plan ahead for such events and always practice preventive maintenance for your car and preventive medicine for your loved one.

Mom's p-c doctor had approved her evaluation, but could he have taken charge and done the evaluation in his office? This is a good example of an inexperience doctor. He should have been questioned about his ability to diagnose dementia and Alzheimer's disease. This was a young doctor who wanted a psychiatrist to do most of the work. Also, check with your supplemental insurance if they will pay for the clinical evaluation.

A caregiver's job is always exciting and demanding. The job requires someone with a lot of courage and a wild assortment of skills. Don't forget, a caregiver's two main jobs: an observer and teacher! Caregivers should teach family members about suspicious accusations and the part they play in the illness. Caregivers have to be tough as nails, but gentle when making deals with Alzheimer's patients. TIP: Wear a helmet all the time! You will be used to wearing it and will look great when you win: "CAREGIVER OF THE YEAR AWARD!"

We believe mom's dad had dementia in his early sixties. He is introduced in the chapter on "fuse boxes." Mom's dad ran several businesses and we were sure he was under a lot of stress all his life. He lived a stressful life with accusations of murder and arrest in the back of his mind. He could lose his family and businesses if he were arrested. It must have been a very stressful life living with early stage Alzheimer's. Grandpa had to be experiencing "suspicion" behavior most of his life. I was told his behavior was hard on the family, caregivers, and employees.

PEOPLE INVOLVED IN COURT CASE

DD   She was the CARE SERVICES advocate who wrote the PO as mom dictated. She came by our home and talked to mom; she never talked to me. Mom was hallucinating when DD interview mom about abusive care. DD admitted to my sister in Houston she never knew or reported mom was wandering late at night. We can guess how accurate DD's "report" was when she admitted not knowing about mom's wandering events.

KC   She was the advocate at ADULT CARE INC. who asked DD to write the abuse charges in PO form and submit to a judge. I was told that KC and Judy, our neighbor, were involved in placing mom into assisted-living without asking permission from any of family members or the staff at the Behavioral Hospital.

PE   The police officer who told KC and DD that I refused to give mom's medicine to him. I told the officer mom was on six tablets and we had only four meds in the house. I gave the ambulance a <u>list</u> of all six meds on a sheet. Instead of the officer reporting this situation to DD and KC, he chose to blame me for the med problems and took things to court. Why can't we blame the ambulance driver who lost the sheet? In court, the judge ask me why I didn't give PE the bottles of meds from our kitchen table.

Caregivers: The Best way to handle this situation is to blame the one who lost the list—the ambulance or fire department! Don't let the police or a judge blame you when your loved one is in a "conglomerate" hospital that doesn't share records with other hospitals.

Keep your attorney's phone number handy so he/she can review any problems 24/7. If it is late, always leave a message when calling attorneys. Most professional people have answering services. Intake Nurses and social workers, especially in Behavior Hospitals know attorneys who work "on the cheap" for caregivers who can do some of the "foot work" for the attorneys. Power of Attorney and Guardianship cost money; Always ask for the number and address of these unsung HEROES!

D EFINITION

ADULT CARE INC. A fictitious name for a group of people who protects abused people by filing PO's for them. The law in my state says if you are a Guardian or have Power of Attorney, the patient can't file a PO on a caregiver. However, happy caregivers aren't going to spend thousand of dollars on attorney fees for these credentials. So, the court will fill up with cases like mine in the future.

ADULT CARE, INC. is not a part of CARE SERVICES. However, someone asked CARE SERVICES to write a Protective Order for mom at the shelter in another county. These so-called "advocates" took statements from a "suspicious" and delusional Alzheimer's patient reporting she lived in a dangerous home. WHAT COULD GO WRONG?

Mom has complained about a dangerous man living in her backyard for over six months. When she discussed the man, I would get a flashlight and take mom and her dogs around the house several times. It isn't a big deal to console loved ones. This dangerous man would come out of the shed at sunset. He would walk around the house several times. Then he looked into her windows and would bang on them. Mom was the only person who could see and hear all of this activity. Sarah, the miniature Schnauzer, often wakes from a deep sleep when leaves falls from a tree, never barked. Moreover, Sarah and Daisy slept with mom but never barked or moved. This incident was the reason our family and the primary-care doctor admitted mom to the Behavioral Hospital. We had to have answers for this strange behavior!

We thought it was some form of hallucination she was experiencing during the dark-winter months. These so-called professionals, DD and KC, took the "bait, hook, line, and sinker." They should have lost their jobs producing such a ridiculous report without calling or questioning her family. Their report was shoddy and wasn't professionally investigated.

My unscientific poll shows the majority of caregivers are more intelligent than advocates about Alzheimer's. In my simple poll, many caregivers were once teachers. Some caregivers owned businesses. Many have advanced degrees. They are caregivers for their loved ones because they want to "give back" for all the things they have accomplished in life.

"DD" wrote the PO for KC because mom was delusional at the time. The judge never asked if the dictation was mom's statements and if she dictated it to DD. I was a caregiver and the court really didn't care what I said! I mentioned to the judge my masters degree in Biology and Chemistry. The elderly judged seem lame at my degrees and only four years as a caregiver.

The "advocates" ran the show and everybody else didn't matter. I would recommend taking an attorney to any court action. The advocates "snickered" when I reported mom had been to the Marcum Hospital's ER three times in two months.

"Aren't we all happy this isn't a murder case?" A Court full of advocates that aren't skilled in Alzheimer's disease, WHAT POSSIBLY COULD GO WRONG? The report for a PO was a short statement from an

Alzheimer's patient experiencing "paranoia" and "suspicion" behavior while dictating to an advocate. How can honest judges allow situations like this occur? One psychologist informed me judges don't know more than they have been told about Alzheimer's: Everyone acts differently with the disease! This is a common definition used by social workers to give to caregivers, police, and the judicial system. It is a definition that seems misused and often misunderstood by everyone hearing it the first time. No one knows what stage an Alzheimer's patient is experiencing at a given time! The first three stages of the disease may not have symptoms even a doctor would recognize. Also, you can't make sense out of "nonsense!"

Mom couldn't write or vocalize a sentenced her last week in the Behavioral Hospital? One test question asked: Write a sentence about any subject. Mom couldn't accomplish the task and tossed her pencil on the table. Furthermore, if an Alzheimer's patient is surrounded by strangers, they can develop hallucinations and paranoia without good reason. Strangers are perceived as being mean, lying, and talking about them. He or she may become suspicious, fearful, and jealous of new people.

Try to understand and console the feeling behind an accusation. I under- stand you are afraid someone wants to hurt you. I am your son and won't let that happen; therefore, I will help keep you safe. TIP: This would be a good time to look through a box of pictures. I kept mom's favorite pictures on the kitchen table where she could look through them when she felt confused or making accusations. For some reason, she liked to look at pictures of her youth, especially baby and toddler pictures. Dementia has made these last six months a sad time. We all thought these pictures verified she was once young and vivacious, but things have changed. The pictures reinforced fond memories of a happy time long ago. I made it a point to kept her baby and toddler pictures separate on the table so visitors could see them and ask a question: "Who are these cute kids?" Honest responses were my goal: "Oh, you were such a cute and a happy baby in Kenwood," Mom's toddler picture is on the front cover of this book.

Mom had forgotten the names of her three kids, but could recall the names of her classmates and friends she knew in her late teens. One caregiver, who lives nearby, told me her mother could recall vivid details about her life at nineteen years old.

In fact, her mother could talk for hours about specific details of her schooling at that early age. However, in the past year, her mother's dementia prevents her from writing a check without help.

Keep several boxes of pictures and a box of their favorite candy in the same area. Russell Stover was mom's favorite and she bought a bag at Wal-Mart on Tuesdays when she did her exercise (shopping). It was easy to monitor her consumption when the candy is individually wrapped— count the empty packages. It was fun to enjoy a few pieces with mom explaining the photos and events depicted. Moreover, I had to place the candy in a large beaker so mom wouldn't overdo it and spoil lunch and dinner. I monitored the candy rappers to keep track of her favorite pieces.

I always cooked a good lunch and dinner each day. She wanted to discontinue Meals-on-Wheelsâ. Breakfast was for her to make to keep her spirits high—usually a doughnut, bagel, or coffee was all she wanted. My goal was a good lunch and dinner before she went to bed. These last six months have been a difficult time because mom's sleep was disturbed by the disease. Mom wanted to get up early, but she always took a nap after lunch or in the late afternoon! The dementia ruined her sleep patterns during the day and at night— napping early in the day made things worse.

She would go to bed at 8 p.m. and wake at 11 p.m. She watched TV until 2 a.m. and slept until 5 a.m. Her doctors, at the Behavioral Hospital, adjusted her sleeping habits and that could have made her despondent some of those days. However, her new sleeping habits didn't seem to bother her that much. Mom had a history of sleeping in the afternoon since her early thirties. We thought it was a bad idea to nap more than four hours in the middle of the day. We agreed a short nap was fine, but anything longer than four hours was questionable for a thirty-year-old mother. My sisters and I never thought much about her naps—mom would just disappear for three hours in the middle of the day. We lived on a ranch so we had things to keep us busy.

Every Wednesday we made a trip to the doughnut shop. My intention was to help mom with breakfast. We loaded the dogs in the back seat and used the drive through to buy a dozen-regular glazed. They were expected to last a week. The doughnut shop was five miles away and she ate five on the way home. She was physically sick by 1:30 p.m. for many of her doctor's appointments.

I tried to schedule all of her appointments on Wednesday afternoons. This schedule helped coordinate activities during the week. I knew not to schedule any outdoor activities on Wednesday because we had appointments. No scenic trip to the lake, no walking the dogs on the shore, and no ducks or geese to feed that day.

TIP: Plan as many activities as you can and make a "weekly" schedule: Alzheimer's patients need to be physically active and have a schedule marked on a calendar.

Flea markets are great places to go in cooler months—leave the dogs in the car. In the summer, lakes and parks have places to walk dogs or let them swim by the shore. Corps Lakes have parks with signs pointing where these activities can or can't be done. Also, look for lakes that have heated- fishing docks and walking paths. Most lakes have "open" fishing docks that are accessible to the handicapped. TIP: Schedule activities so mom/dad can read them from the calendar. This helps encourage participation!

Place lawn chairs and an ice chest in the trunk. Enjoy lakes and parks between 7-9 a.m. when it is coolest. If parts of the lake are closed to dogs, visit other lakes and parks. Scheduled parks and lakes for Fridays!

TIP: Don't forget the loaf of bread for ducks and geese. Also, keep dogs on leashes all the time! Finally, this would be a good time to ask for a FREE "Golden-Age Card." This card allows a 50% reduction in fees at U.S. Army Corps of Engineer Lakes. The pay booth at the entrance of parks can issue the card. It takes only a few minutes and the card is a lifetime reduction in fees. If grandma is sixty-five and in the car, the car enjoys a reduce fee.

Mom started eating sweets again and we had a hard time slowing her down! The doctor wanted her to gain a few extra pounds so he wasn't worried about her diet. He gave her a prescription for increasing her appetite. I thought she would gain weight eating all that sugar, but she didn't. I asked the young doctor if the medication was necessary because I was having an awful time giving five pills a day. "I am against this extra pill," I told the doctor. I did see positive results from the medication—she would eat well over half of the doughnuts on Wednesday morning instead of her usual three or four.

I bought some fresh fruit and slowly changed her eating habits at the lake. The fresh-sliced fruit came pre-packaged and was a good diet change. I found a variety of fresh-cut fruit in the produce section of the grocery store. Her doctor okayed the fruit as a healthy alternative to take to the lake.

We always took the dogs to be groomed to make them look like show dogs on Tuesdays. That was a good day because it was a slow day. Mom had stopped driving after "I lost all of her car keys." She wanted to go with me to pick them up when Scott was done. Scott told me a recent story about mom: "Your mother called about Daisy's grooming last month." She said, "Daisy's trim was the worst job I have ever done." She asked, "You must have someone new working for you?" Scott replied, "No, Ms. Dollie I have done all the grooming for the last 23-years." Scott said he had worried about mom's mental health for some time, but didn't say anything.

He said, "Ms Dollie called me back in about an hour and complimented my grooming Sarah and Daisy. Scott told me mom apologized and told him, "You did an excellent job on both dogs. She said it was the best job ever!"

I told Scott that mom wanted to cuss you out, but I persuaded her to drop the idea! Scott works cheap and others charge twice as much. You had better leave him alone because if he drops you, the closest grooming is twelve miles. Scott laughed at the story and said, "Yeah, that's Ms. Dollie."

I noticed a strange thing occur six weeks after mom changed her new primary-care doctor. She was tired of him for some reason and wanted another. She said her trust in him was gone because he helped put her in the Behavioral Hospital. I ask, "What concerns do you have about your p-c doctor?" She said, "I think he has damaged my reputation and I can't do anything about it." I almost burst out laughing, but held my laughter to hear more! She continued, "I think he has damaged me and I don't think we can do anything." I told her, "Well, if you want to change doctors, let me know as soon as possible so they can send us a list of doctors! She replies, "I'm "trash" to my friends and they think you should have been in the clinic instead of me!

I could see where she was going and said, "Let's ask your insurance company for a woman doctor this time." Maybe, a woman doctor will give you more "respect" than your present doctor. Always plan ahead for a change in doctors because Alzheimer's patients may become suspicious of him/her and ask for a new one.

Call the insurance company for dates for changing doctors and ask for a list of doctors. TIP: Try to get a doctor that is close to home. A short travel time is a valuable thing for some Alzheimer's patients. Do you want a male or female doctor? Young or old? My personal opinion is to select same- gender doctor. It is easy to find a woman doctor and many women prefer one for obvious reasons. I asked for a woman doctor after she complained about her first doctor's clinic and how far it was to travel.

Unfortunately, the doctor refused to take mom because she had met her quota for adding seniors that year. Mom never mentioned changing doctors again and eventually that request was cancelled. At times, mom was on her doctor's case for something she hated, and other times she praised the man as the best doctor in town. A gender change might be all your loved one needs for a "fresh" start!

CH. 3 PARANOIA COMES TO TOWN

If you haven't experienced "paranoia" behavior in a relative with dementia, its appearance could change your mind being a caregiver.

An Alzheimer's patients acts like a child "snitching" on a friend. All of a sudden, your loved one accuses you of stealing things out of his/ her bank account or a drawer at home. The Alzheimer's mind will make the accusations in your presence; they have no qualms repeating it to strangers.

Their mind seems to spew statements that hinge on negative views and void of emotion. The paranoid behavior is scary and disturbing the first time you witness its puzzling "nonsense." It is in "suspicion stage" of Alzheimer's, the naïve and untrained should back away. Only psychiatrists, trained psychologists, and medical doctors should venture into its muddy waters.

Unfortunately, the untrained can be found splashing around in the puddle of "nonsense." I asked the advocate, who wrote the PO, about her educational background. She replied, "I have a Master's degree in social relations." I wanted to say, "Miss, that is not enough education to scrape the surface for clues in Alzheimer's disease. A patient being afraid of people in and around their home is most likely paranoid and requires more education and experience than you possess! Also, I wanted her to hypothesize about a personal dilemma: "Your level of education can't make sense out of "NONSENSE?"

I knew a man whose wife would undress and sneak away at the same time each day— shortly after dark. She was in her early sixties and was fortunate to live in the country where homes were far apart. Her husband was young enough to locate her before she attracted the attention of neighbors. The doctor diagnosed her as having a urinary tract infection. The doctor's diagnosis wasn't complete! However, she had problems holding a job and the family worried her problems might be dementia and psychosis.

Her doctor took her off most of her drugs. She wandered nude again and again and refused to believe her family. They told her, "Yes, you did run naked in the dark!" Friends of the family politely told Anna about the tattoo of a feather on her "butt." She never knew her wandering was a problem, but no one knew she had dementia until a year later. Her dementia made her life more dangerous causing the family to focus on Alzheimer's.

It's common for a person with dementia to wander and/or become lost. In fact, more than 60 percent of individuals with Alzheimer's will wander at some point. They may try to go home when already there or attempt to recreate a familiar routine, such as going to school or work.

As the disease progresses, the person with dementia will need increased supervision. At some point, it will no longer be safe for him or her to be left alone.[4]

In early December, mom asked me to take her to the bank. She wanted some cash on hand for the holidays. I had placed $200 in cash in her purse a few weeks earlier because she was hinting that money was missing from her purse. I said, "Okay, but don't get too much because you have quite a lot in the corner of your coin purse. She walked up to the teller and accused me of stealing her debit card from her purse. She told the teller that J.P. withdrew a lot of cash from her account in the last month. All I could do was smile and shake my head back and forth at the teller. Mom never asked if I borrowed any money from her purse. It was an accusation that had to be made in front of others for mom to be emotionally relieved.

The teller knew mom because she was in the bank just last week to order a new debit card. She had lost her card for the second time in two days. This was actually the third order for a debit card in the last month. I felt ashamed listening to her inform the teller hundreds of dollars were missing from her purse. Finally, we knew mom was paranoid, so I asked the bank-account rep to investigate the matter. "How much cash has been withdrawn in the last six weeks on her debit card?" After a few minutes on her computer, the rep looked at my mother, and sadly said, "None!"

Memory loss and confusion may cause a person with Alzheimer's to perceive things in new and unusual ways. Individuals may become suspicious of those around them, even accusing others of theft, infidelity or other improper behavior. Sometimes a person may misinterpret what he or she sees and hears.[5]

Mom could have been accusing someone of poisoning her medicine or food. Also, it could have been an accusation that I wasn't really her son. She could have accused me of not taking care of her or didn't know me. Mom drifted in and out of suspicion behavior with poisoning her medicine. On one occasion, she thought the doctor was working with me to poison her with medications. She told neighbors that a Mexican man was living in her house with J.P. and me. "He scares me," she told neighbors and ER staff.

These accusations can be embarrassing and a nightmare for caregivers. Caregivers need to prepare themselves for these situations.

TIP: Place some money in the purse/wallet and remind them they don't need to go to the bank today. This is common in Alzheimer's patients and if you hear them say money is missing from their purse/wallet, immediately put some cash in the purse/wallet. Buy another wallet or purse like the one they own and place cash inside. You can prevent the "snitching!"

TIP: I would go to the bank and get $100 in ten-dollar bills and fold the bills in half and place the "wad" into her purse. It looked full of cash and did the trick. A wallet/purse full of cash is an easy way to prevent "snitching." THE CASH IS WORTH EVERY DIME! It is easier to give cash than fight a Protective Order in court! These paranoid stories were believed by so-called "professionals" without hesitation! WHY IS THE LEGAL SYSTEM BROKEN?

I motioned to my mother, "Let's go, the bank will send your new debit card in a few days." Mom started discussing something new with the account rep: "J.P. makes me keep my purse on the kitchen chair and I don't want it in the kitchen. People walk through the kitchen all day, you wouldn't believe all the people walking through the kitchen." I said, "Okay Mom, she has to order your card and help others in the bank. We will go home and wait for your debit card to come in the mail. We thanked the rep for all the time she spent helping a patient with suspicion behavior.

Mom was paranoid most of January. She would catch me working on the computer and ask, "Who are all of these people walking through the house? I don't want my purse on the back of a chair —someone will steal it and I want have any money in the house. "Okay, put your purse in your bedroom." I replied. The paranoia has no good reason and caregivers shouldn't spend a lot of time worrying about why it occurs. Caregivers need to treat symptoms as they occur and we rely on doctors to do the rest.

None of us could think of a reason mom was paranoid the first part of January. Some guessed she could be recalling her guests at Christmas. Most of her guests hadn't seen her in years and could be considered "strangers" in her mind. The consensus was mom experienced some sort of flashback from all these strangers that visited at Christmas. Also, mom gave away some of her possessions at that time. Removing property by her grandkids could have triggered suspicion behavior.

We lose a large number of caregivers in situations like mine. I will never take a caregiver job again for anyone! I would hesitate to take a caregiver job even if I had Power of Attorney or Guardianship. I don't trust the courts to make good decisions in any Alzheimer's cases! Court was awful and disrespectful to my family and me.

These so-called professionals: KC, DD, PE, Care Services, and two judges were all professionals that were quick to make sense out of "nonsense!"

I mentioned two judges because KC asked DD to write the PO. However, they asked an "initial" judge to okay the PO without any proof of abuse. This would seem to be stepping on a caregiver's civil rights. But, this book proves no one cares about caregivers! None of these people, including the two judges, knew the first thing about the disease. However, they were quick to talk about Alzheimer's in court, but said very little for me to offer a teaching moment!

Caregivers shouldn't fall for the excuse many police officers and social workers use: We did it to "err on the side of caution!" No one knows what that statement means and don't try to explain it, because you can't. It is similar to the word: FREEZE! I am an Award-Winning Chemist but I don't have the slightest idea what "freeze" means in police jargon! If an officer sent my mother to a safe house to "err on the side of caution," a better choice would be to take her to a hospital where she is still considered a patient and has a behavior contract to honor. To "err on the side of caution" is always "subjective." In my opinion, it is a free pass for an officer or advocate that knows little about a disease or recent hospitalization.

In Community Policing, let's do away with "erratic jargon" and statements. Turn everything over to doctors and psychiatrists. Let our best professionals decide what's best for mom and stop all this "erring" by those who know little about mother's dementia. Let's stop the practice of placing dementia patients into nursing homes at Stage 3 of the disease!

Alzheimer's is a fatal disease and needs more respect by all professionals. CARE SERVICES is going to wake up someday and find a huge shortage of caregivers in this state. I have heard attorneys say it was already critical with more laws ahead. It's their own fault not paying attention to what they are doing. I observed a careless bunch of people in my case. Directors were so out-of-touch with their employees—visiting with directors was similar to talking to a small child about a toy they had last year! I wanted to ask the directors if they ever fired anyone for incompetence. However, the phone conversation was so immature, I just hung up on them.

It isn't hard to tell someone working for the state they do a poor job. I visited with bosses about built-in problems, but employees were allowed to continue sloppy work. I constantly asked nurses and social workers:

Do you ever attempt to call the caregiver or the family member of the patient experiencing paranoid behavior? TIP: It isn't a pretty sight if you run into problems caring for your loved one in my state. I was never contacted until I got the summons to appear in court! WHAT KIND OF CARE SERVICE DOES THAT? I carried papers from one of the most respected hospitals in my state with a diagnosis of dementia. One Police Captain had the nerve to suggest: "Have you ever thought of getting a second opinion?" I immediately said, "No!"

This documentation and days of testing satisfied our family and friends. Mom's dad and mother had dementia and my memory of their disease was still clear in my mind. I wasn't going to hire another clinic to report dementia with Lewy bodies.

I would rename this department: CARELESS-CARE SERVICES. If you try to get help, you will be thrown into a WILD CIRCUS and they will spin you into oblivion. "GOOD LUCK TO CAREGIVERS REQUESTING HELP FROM YOUR STATE!"

Mom stopped smiling at her mistakes. She was never seen laughing at anything funny on TV. Her smile was gone and we may never see it again!

She liked to wash dishes but always needed help starting the machine. She stared at the machine for several minutes. I could tell she had forgotten the sequence of buttons to push—it took four buttons, pushed in the correct sequence, to start the washer. TIP: If you make dishwashers, change the system to as few buttons as necessary to start the machine. And, make sure the buttons are as large as you can make them. A "crank type" switch is ideal and some washer companies make them. Thanks from all the caregivers in the country for a large-starting switch!

After the dishes dried in the washer, I watched her take the utensil tray from the washer and dump the entire tray into the drawer. Instead of sorting the forks and spoons, she dumped all the utensils together. I couldn't keep from laughing; She never sorted utensils again, but she did watch me sort them. Finally, I asked if I could do the dishes once in a while and she said that's okay with me!

I believe some of the negative views coming from Alzheimer's patients are the result of the loss of memory. Also, I think it is directly related to the amount of activity and stimulation in their daily lives. Mom tried doing word puzzles of all kinds to stimulate her mind. She worked feverishly on puzzles for over a year and stopped suddenly. I saw new puzzle books near her "big chair." The puzzle books were starting to confuse her and I could see they were becoming an irritant. The irritation and anxiety was enough to ruin her day. I placed them in a sack and took them to the trash. I never heard a word about puzzle books.

Mom refused to walk like most of her friends. Both doctors were aggressive in their efforts to get her walking. She wasn't a physically active person during her teens or adult life. I always thought if she had been more active, her dementia could have been prevented or arrested. Even on trips to the lake, she resisted walking short distances with Sarah and Daisy. I always grabbed the dog's leashes and let them walk in front of us.

Walking is an excellent form of exercise for the elderly. It can improve circulation, digestion, and attitude in the elderly. Start with walking the dog and increase the distance over time. Always ask your doctor before starting an exercise plan for your loved one. Mom liked to shop at Wal-Mart and Target every Tuesday. She added at least 1/4 mile or more of great exercise. Pushing a cart stabilized her gait and made the exercise safer and more fun. Mom got so tired that she couldn't remember the fat guy who pounded on her bedroom windows every night. Most stores have a snack bar for shoppers. I made sure we stopped and had a snack so Mom and I could finish our exercising. An ER doctor suggested mom visit each room in her house three times a day; I recall that idea was turned down. Therefore, Wal-Mart and Target provided a place for her to exercise in the winter months.

My grandpa's electrician job kept him physically active into his seventies. We always thought his physically-active jobs slowed Alzheimer's so he could experience a longer and healthy life.

Friday's trip to the lake turned into visiting while sitting in the car. The dogs were restless and wanted to walk the shore and chase ducks. We could tell by her attitude and behavior that Tuesday was going to be mom's best day of the week. The exercise on Tuesday, walking behind a cart for thirty minutes, made a world of difference in her motivation and spirits for the rest of the week.

TIP: If you need a few good days, take your loved one shopping on Mondays. I scheduled shopping for Tuesdays because it was always a slow day for businesses.

CH. 4 WHAT IS ALZHEIMER'S

Dr. Alois Alzheimer, a German physician, first described the disease in 1906. His patients had a history of memory problems, confusion, and difficulty understanding questions.

Dr. Alzheimer's autopsies discovered a pattern of twisted bands of fibers (tangles) and dense deposits surrounding the nerve cells (plaques). When both the plaques and tangles are found during an autopsy, the diagnosis is Alzheimer's. In 1906, the average lifespan in United States was about 50 years. Few people reached the age of greatest risk. As a result, the disease was considered rare and attracted little scientific interest. The present average life expectancy of 78 years has changed the focus of research.

Today, Alzheimer's is at the front of biomedical research, with 90 percent of what we know discovered in the last 20 years.

Alzheimer's is a disease of the brain that causes problems with memory, thinking, and behavior. It is not a normal part of aging. Alzheimer's gets worse over time. Although symptoms can vary widely, the first problem many people notice is forgetfulness severe enough to affect their ability to function at home and work, or to enjoy lifelong hobbies. The disease may cause a person to become confused, lost in familiar places, misplace things or have trouble with language. It can be easy to explain away unusual behavior as part of normal aging, especially for someone who seems physically healthy. Any concerns about memory loss should be discussed with a doctor.[6]

Alzheimer's is not a normal part of aging, although the greatest known risk factor is increasing age, and the majority of people with Alzheimer's are 65 and older. But Alzheimer's is not just a disease of old age. Up to 5 percent of people with the disease have early-onset Alzheimer's, which often appears when someone is in their 40s or 50s.

Alzheimer's is the sixth leading cause of death in the United States. Those with Alzheimer's live an average of eight years after their symptoms become noticeable to others, but survival can range from four to 20 years, depending on age and other health conditions.

Alzheimer's has no current cure, but treatments for symptoms are available and research continues. Although current Alzheimer's treatments cannot stop Alzheimer's from progressing, they can temporarily slow the worsening of dementia symptoms and improve quality of life for those with Alzheimer's and their caregivers.

The most common early symptom of Alzheimer's is difficulty remembering newly learned information. Just like the rest of our bodies, our brains change as we age. Most of us eventually notice some slowed thinking and occasional problems with remembering certain things. However, serious memory loss, confusion, and other changes in the way our minds work may be a sign that brain cells are failing. As Alzheimer's advances through the brain it leads to increasingly severe symptoms, including disorientation, mood, and behavior changes; deepening confusion about events, time, and place; unfounded suspicions about family, friends, and professional caregivers; more serious memory loss and behavior changes; and difficulty speaking, swallowing, and walking.

People with memory loss or other signs of Alzheimer's may find it hard to recognize they have a problem. Signs of dementia may be more obvious to family members or friends. Anyone experiencing dementia-like symptoms should see a doctor as soon as possible. Early diagnosis and intervention methods are improving dramatically, and treatment options and sources of support can improve quality of life.

There is no single test that proves a person has Alzheimer's. The workup is designed to evaluate overall health and identify any conditions that could affect how well the mind is working. When other conditions are ruled out, the doctor can then determine if it is Alzheimer's or another dementia. Experts estimate that a skilled physician can diagnose Alzheimer's with more than 90 percent accuracy. Physicians can almost always determine that a person has dementia, but it may sometimes be difficult to determine the exact cause.[7]

CH. 5 JUDGES AND POLICE LACK TRAINING

Mom was incoherent when she left home to go to he ER that final night. She was paranoid when she told the ER staff she was in danger at home. Informing the ER staff that her four kids lived in California is proof of her being delusional that night. TIP: Judges, police officers, nurses, and social workers know even less about the disease than caregivers. In court, the judge looked at me and said, "Alzheimer's patients act differently with the disease." I held my laughter the best I could under the circumstances.

Further, I thought about responding to the judge: If patients act differently, how will you ever make a decision in a case? But, I knew this judge probably spent state money for a workshop about the disease. I wasn't going to burst his bubble in front of his colleagues, but I thought about educating him while I had the chance!

Judges, police, caregivers, and social workers need to understand that suspicious accusations are a part of the illness. It's similar to having the flu, you are going to cough sometime during the disease—coughing is part of the disease. Likewise, during Alzheimer's disease you will likely hear outrageous accusations about someone—that is part of the disease!

Without curiosity, you are truly "up a creek without a paddle." People go through life with little or no curiosity about their work can't do a good job.

Further, if caregivers aren't "eager to know" about Alzheimer's they are wasting their time. Please, if you don't have curiosity about Alzheimer's, do your loved one a favor and resign!

Perhaps these so-called experts selected the wrong career. I see people in the wrong career all the time. They are the incompetent ones we all know and complain. A "flood" of incompetent people were found in my case. No curiosity was noticed in the court for the advocates who wrote the PO. I had no choice but to file complaints at the State Capitol! However, they probably thought they were the hardest Alzheimer's workers in the county. Caregivers must educate themselves to build more curiosity. That curiosity will produce a better environment for our loved ones who have this tragic disease.

I knew a teacher who worked so hard she was exhausted at the end of the day. She had a hard time walking to her car to drive home. In class she did everything for the kids. She would run to the corner, where she kept all the science equipment, and got the equipment for them. She explained things over and over. At the end of the day, she was about to drop.

I politely suggested she make the kids work as hard as she did in class. After my suggestion, she improved her curiosity for teaching and turned out to be a great science teacher!

Judges, strangers, and police are the worst of the bunch simply because their "training" limits the amount of curiosity. The answer is as simple as not being properly trained. Judges who make silly decisions will continue to make stupid decisions and it will harm future caregivers. Judges are not helpful to caregivers and it doesn't take long to see such disrespect in court. I eventually signed a petition after my court appearance to remove the judge from the bench. Large organizations are watching our rights "closer to home" than ever before. I recommend writing your state rep. for help. Describe what happened in a simple letter and include statements that back up your complaint. These people can change the laws if they hear from us.

Judges, strangers, and police officers know one fact about dementia: Dementia is slow and predictable! The judge stated, "There will be plenty of time to obtain guardianship! This illogical opinion is going to be a thorn in the neck of caregivers. Finally, when feelings erupt that no one cares about caregiver's, the curiosity is gone and so are the caregivers! Who takes care of grandma/grandpa? I often wondered if the elderly judge might have the disease due to his malicious court.

I think the only solution is to create a "family-court" where judges deal only with Alzheimer's cases. Also, I think special judges should be trained "now" so caregivers can be given special attention in court before it is too late. The court is presently a place to throw stones and mock caregivers. Yes, I lost my civil rights in our court system and it wasn't something this veteran was proud to witness.

If you think judges and advocates are up-to-date on this disease, don't kid yourself! My case is a good example of how professionals are out-of-touch with Alzheimer's disease. And, that should be a warning for everyone reading this book—many of you will reach the estimated lifespan of 78. You may need a caregiver even if you don't have dementia. We have a right to cheap caregivers if we reach that expected lifespan. Caregivers are going to refuse to work with Alzheimer's patients after reading a few books about the judicial abuse and bad laws.

Being a caregiver can be a neat, full-time job working for Alzheimer's patients. The caregiver can't get the disease and the elderly try to please most helpers that come into their lives. If we don't have a steady supply of caregivers with more authority, eventually the number of caregivers will dry up! If a caregiver has Power of Attorney or Guardianship, the patient can't file a PO in my state. I wake up nights with thoughts that a caregiver will get a summons to appear in "traffic court" for so-called Alzheimer's abuse.

The activity of disrespecting "caregivers" is occurring now, but we call it regular court appearance. We don't have time to wait for money to be appropriated for this disease. In my new system, judges will not have court in a regular courthouse. Courthouse will be rooms set aside in clinics and hospitals with doctors and social workers. This new court will rid itself of social workers and advocates that have agendas against caregivers.

Social workers and advocates that have multiple complaints filed against them cannot attend this court. Complaints will regulate who keeps his job in my ALZHEIMER'S COURT. I discovered by accident, one social worker in my case, had so many complaints against her, she was called a "walking-crime wave!" Please God, we don't need incompetent social workers anywhere near our new HOSPITAL COURT! In my PO case, I caught doctors and nurses willing to pass the buck. They didn't have any "curiosity" for the disease, my mother, or her caregiver. They must have had lots of hate to write a PO. To the advocates: Hating caregivers isn't part of your job. The same advice is offered to both ADULT CARE, INC. and CARE SERVICES.

During the editing of this book, I got a chance to listen to a great Chief of Police. He reminded new officers that our job is to "HELP" people and not to antagonize a situation—similar to the oath doctors take! Remember, we are not judges we are "HELP OFFICERS."

Alzheimer's disease will require many people with high levels of curiosity, energy, and a willing to "help" patients. The volume of caregivers will have to be staggering in order to help treat and care for dementia patients. I see my state losing this race for large numbers of happy caregivers for our loved ones. Shipping mom to a nursing home at Stage 3 Alzheimer's is reckless for the state, patient, caregiver, and society. It is the home where they feel safe and secure.

If we can't find a cure for Alzheimer's, some dementia patients will have to live on the streets or in run-down-storage buildings. We don't have the curiosity to build thousands of nursing homes for this deadly disease. It is a sad outlook for Alzheimer's disease if no cure is found. The future for this disease seems grim because the lifespan should continually rise for humans. Remember, I don't claim to be a soothsayer. However, I plan to fight for a nation of happy caregivers for our loved ones.

CH. 6 "EASY" DIAGNOSIS?

Physicians can almost always determine that a person has dementia, but it may sometimes be difficult to determine the exact cause. Autopsy studies are used to determine those with Alzheimer's and dementias.

Research shows that older Latinos are about one-and-a-half times as likely as older whites to have Alzheimer's and other dementias. Older African-Americans are about twice as likely to have Alzheimer's and other dementias as older whites. The reason for these differences is not well understood, but researchers believe that higher rates of vascular disease in these groups may also put them at greater risk for developing Alzheimer's.[8]

The following steps are used diagnosing Alzheimer's:

1. Understanding the problem.
2. What kind of symptoms have occurred
3. When they began
4. How often they happen
5. If they have gotten worse

The doctor will interview the person being tested and others close to him or her to gather information about current and past mental and physical illnesses. It is helpful to bring a list of all the medications the person is taking. The doctor will also obtain a history of key medical conditions affecting other family members, especially whether they may have or had Alzheimer's disease or other dementias.

Mental status testing evaluates memory, the ability to solve simple problem and other thinking skills. The testing gives an overall sense of whether the person is aware of symptoms and knows the date, time and where he or she is. Can remember a short list of words, following instructions and do simple calculations.

A physician will: Evaluate diet and nutrition. Check blood pressure, temperature and pulse. Listen to the heart and lungs. Perform other procedures to assess overall health. The physician will collect blood and urine samples and may order other laboratory tests. Information from these tests can help identify disorders such as anemia, infection, diabetes, kidney disease, certain vitamin deficiencies, thyroid abnormalities, and problems with the heart, blood vessels or lungs. All of these conditions may cause confused thinking, trouble focusing attention, memory problems or other symptoms similar to dementia. A doctor will closely evaluate the person for problems that may signal brain disorders other than Alzheimer's.

The physician will also test: Reflexes, coordination, muscle tone and strength, eye movement, speech, and sensation. The doctor is looking for signs of small or large strokes, Parkinson's disease, brain tumors, fluid accumulation on the brain and other illnesses that may impair memory or thinking.[9]

My mother gave her kids only a small number of hints she was having problems with her memory. Forgetting the kids' names was common. Mom had a history of memory problems that goes back to her thirties. She complained her memory was bad beginning in her thirties. She told me it was difficult to keep it a secret. She was caught forgetting new information as early as thirty years old. She mentioned, "I never wanted to go to college because of my poor memory!"

However, losing things like her purse, keys, checks, and debit cards were recent events in life. She would be upset all day if she lost her purse. We helped look for a purse for hours before finding it hanging in the closet. The second time she lost her purse, we found it under the bed.

TIP: Lost objects are never found in a logical locations.

Mom's young doctor always began each visit with a short-mental test. "What day and time is it," Ms. Dollie? Ms. Dollie, "I want you remember three words for me." He would give them slowly and then he would say, "remember these for later." Then, the doctor wanted to know, "what country she was living. He ask, "What is your address and who is president?" Finally, the doctor ask mom to draw a clock with hands showing the time for 12:30 p.m. placing the small and large hands in their correct location. I believe the president and her address were the only correct answers. We believed mom had drifted into Stage 3 after this last office test. This office visit was six weeks before she took her last ER trip.

I think some questions were related to her "friends" and their dislike for President Obama. She and her friends never could tell me why they disliked the President. I think is was a "generation thing" they held from their youth. Mom knew the president question each time it was asked. She and her dad always had an interest in politics. Grandpa ran for State Rep. when he was in his late forties.

Grandpa's memory was questionable and his kids knew he had problems. I remember he asked for help when electrical situations turned complex and technical. He would talk to himself, "I am going to need Don Cox all week." When he needed Don Cox, I knew he was having memory problems and I was careful to pay close attention during the week. Don was my uncle and was considered an expert electrician.

CH. 7 WANDERING-BY-AMBULANCE?

Caregivers should understand that wandering-by-ambulance is not only dangerous for the patient, but is equally dangerous to caregivers. My case is a good example of what can legally happen to an unsuspecting caregiver. In the event the patient has lied to the ambulance driver and has made it to the hospital, you still can't relax! The hospital is likely seeing your loved one for the first time. If you are with your loved one, you still need to be on guard at the hospital. This is dementia; it is not a stroke. The ER may not be your friend, they aren't there to diagnose dementia or Alzheimer's disease. And, they likely don't have your loved one's health records. The ER doctors, without records, are in the simple diagnosis mode—they start at a disadvantage! Your p-c doctor can listen to dad's aches, pains, and complaints, but the ER environment should be all business. Your job is to introduce yourself and explain why you brought grandma/grandpa to the ER. The admitting nurse will document the reason for grandma presence and pass the information to the ER Staff.

DEFINITION

MRI: Magnetic resonance imaging. Images produced by these machines can look at the brain for tumors, bleeding in the brain, nerve injury, and damaged caused by a stroke. MRI can also find problems of the eye and optic nerves, and the ears and auditory nerve.

Please remember that some hospitals aren't sharing health records. My mother had no physical illness and the ER staff didn't do anything to find me. The ER staff is not likely looking for caregivers or guardians if your loved one has no physical illness. And, your questions about medications, comments, and procedures should be in a small notebook for your loved one's safety. Most ER's provide Exit INFO for caregivers so they know what was diagnosed and what to do in the future. Caregivers should keep these papers and any notes in a safe place for review! I saved them in a manila folder marked ER. A caregiver must report all ER visits to the primary-care doctor as soon as possible. I always used Wednesdays for follow-ups for wanderings and trips to the ER's.

Some elderly patients like the attention of an ambulance ride, and will abuse the situation. Write the date, time, and reason for trips to the hospital in your notebook—eventually add the information to your computer!

Heart attacks and strokes can identify themselves by chest pain, dizziness, slurred words, and falling to the ground. Trips to the ER were never questioned by me; I knew when mom was faking a stroke or abdominal pain. The ER was always slow during the night and mom got a ride any time she wanted.

A nurse politely mentioned that if I could find a family member who was willing to take a "firm" approach to mom's wandering, it could prevent a tragedy. I didn't want a relative yelling and screaming at mom so I decided to nix the idea.

One ER doctor had the courtesy to look for me during an ER visit. This visit was the second ER visit in one week and at 11:30 p.m. I checked mom's blood pressure on the home unit and it was 198/99. I took her to the ER; in the hospital is was 148/89. They reminded me the value isn't a serious problem for someone her age. The doctors seemed upset treating an elderly woman for that kind of pressure. They waited three hours to see if the pressure would go down. This was the same ER we were asked not to use by her supplemental-insurance company.

Mom's high-blood pressure turned out to be normal for someone her age, so they planned to release her at 2:30 a.m. I walked to the ER parking lot to get my cell phone. I sat in the hospital's waiting room watching a rerun of a NBA game to stay awake. Don't expect doctors and nurses to search long for guardians or caregivers. By the way, when the ER doctor found me in the waiting room at 2 a.m. drinking coffee, he asked: "Why was your mother brought to the emergency room? We can't find anything wrong with your mother and I am releasing her!" I told the ER doctor mom was experiencing symptoms of high-blood pressure on our home monitor. I thought she was hallucinating about the "fat man" causing the high-blood pressure, but it turned out to be an over-the-counter-pain pill she took earlier in the day. The ER staff checked her blood pressure several times and readings were slightly above normal. The doctor gave her a 10-mg Lisinopril tablet and waited for her pressure to stabilize at 128/78. She was released with special INFO: "The blood-pressure unit at home must be replaced!"

Mom had been taking analgesics for about a week for tooth surgery and pain. Doctors thought the pain pills caused her pressure to rise suddenly. The common analgesic push her blood pressure to high levels and caused her to take Lisinopril (blood pressure medicine) for almost two weeks. I said, "Okay, its late, I'll take her home!"

On a third ER visit, the admitting nurse wanted mom to answer questions on the initial forms. She reminded me not to say anything and let my mother answer all the questions. The nurse politely said, "Let your mother answer on her own!" I didn't know at the time, but she was being checked for coherency. Mom was having abdominal problems, cramping, and a headache at 12:30 a.m.

The supplemental-insurance company called that same day. They advised us not to use this ER until further notice. The insurance company was still having trouble billing from the new hospital. I promised the insurance rep. that we wouldn't use the ER again.

The insurance company was communicating with the hospital and me on a regular basis. The supplemental-insurance company seemed to have an enormous task recovering paperwork and bills from the new hospital. I had no idea the paperwork was in such a mess. "I will take her to a different ER on the next trip,"

I promised.Mom is sick and it is close to home, so we tried it once more. All three ER visits to this hospital included MRI's showing mom never had a major stroke in her life. However, specialists tell me that mini-stokes are like "snakes in the grass" on a MRI—they are hard to see, if at all. Therefore, mom's three trips to the ER proved she didn't have a history of "major strokes." She had manipulated the ER doctors on those three occasions without their knowledge.

Five days after being released from the Behavioral Hospital, mom took her "next-to-last" ambulance ride to the same Behavioral Hospital ER. She signed in at 5:16 p.m. Mom was using "severe-abdominal pain" as a way to wander-by-ambulance. She ignored her Safety Agreement by not informing the ER doctors she was to be transferred to the Behavioral Hospital. I thought about driving her to the admissions office after they finished with her diagnosis. I changed my mind and ask the nurse to load her into my car. I didn't admit her that night because I was so tired from hiking all day and she wanting to go home and sleep in her bed! However, I reported the ER trip the following day to her primary-care doctor and asked for his support. I got the doctor's permission to hike and fish and the doctor seem to think she was still in Stage 2 Alzheimer's (early stage) and it was okay to leave her by herself since I had the car keys locked in the safe.

Four days later, I visited the Heart Hospital that called the Sheriff and let him do a locked-down at the hospital. I wanted to hear their side of the story. I had a cordial interview at the hospital. However, the hospital refused to let me see the final diagnosis. I had a good idea that anything the hospital had written on this sheet was false or could be scrutinized. This last visit to a ER showed she was complaining about a stroke. I glanced at the sheet and could see a reference to stroke. The hospital refused to let me read the entire ER form or the results of my recent complaint. The hospital refused to answer questions about mom's health. The hospital wasn't told mom was a dementia patient. I complained to the Hospital CEO and he ask me, four months later, if mom was a dementia patient. I filed an official complaint with the hospital CEO when I found out the deputy failed to provide that bit of information to the ER. The Sheriff didn't provide any information to the ER after finding mom in our neighborhood on two occasions. The supplemental-insurance company wanted to file on my behalf and commented, "They should have called you before calling the Sheriff."

A heart specialist, who was a family friend, informed me that mom didn't have a stroke or she would have been placed on blood thinners for a period of time. Therefore, I believe she got her standard treatment consisting of one pill on her tongue for nausea. This is another example of "suspicion behavior" at work. I could see a pattern developing: She was using hospital ER's to manipulate the staff so she could stay overnight in a safe place far from the "fat man!" Doctors consistently diagnosed nausea for mother when she arrived complaining of abdominal pains or strokes. I thought about filing Medicare Fraud against the Heart Hospital, but decided not to harass them and referred everything to my attorney.

My mother was, all of a sudden, in a quandary because she couldn't get the hospitals to keep her overnight for any health complaint. Each ER visit cost the insurance a total of $3,000. Thank God her insurance company had enough insight to contemplate the elderly abusing hospital ER's. The elderly can and do manipulate doctors and staff. An attorney told me, "she was smarter than the doctors; however, mom's dementia prevented her from remembering all the tricks that had failed in the past." She must have thought of a good plan, or a friend did it for her, to stay in the hospital by accusing me of some sort of abuse.

Finally, I would recommend caregivers keep your loved one busy with toddler puzzles. Small picture puzzles are great! Don't buy one with 1,000 pieces; thirty pieces may be too much. Spend time in the toy section of a store and buy decks of cards. My favorite place was a local "learning store" in the neighborhood. If you don't know where they are located, call a first- grade teacher at the local elementary school. Mom got tired of word puzzles so don't buy more than your loved one will use. Before hanging up, ask the teacher where they buy their supplies. Education-supply companies will sell anything in their catalog to the public. Ward's Scientific® is highly recommended by teachers and caregivers. Ward's catalog is online—look for puzzles for first-graders or elementary supplies. I bought five beakers online for ten dollars. The largest beaker was about a gallon in size and the smallest was about two cups. Mom and I had a lot of fun with these plastic measuring devices. I had mom place her Russell Stover candy in one container and pills found on the floor in another. These discarded pills were dangerous for Sarah and Daisy; the pills reminded mom of what not to do!

Keep mom active by visiting the Senior-Citizen Center. On the way home, ask her/him if they enjoyed the Center. If they did, go more often and help introduce them to new people. The elderly develop patterns in retirement, so plan to go to the Senior Citizen's Center at certain times each week so she/he can get acquainted with the same people. If she/he can't remember their names, take your notebook and use a cell-phone picture and record names. Perhaps they will remember the same people they saw last week.

TIP: If your loved one doesn't like a particular group of senior citizens, go at different times and ask someone which group has similar personalities. I discovered if I took mom once a month she enjoyed the stay more than going several times a month. Mark the calendar for an activity they enjoy when they attend the Senior Citizen's Center.

CH. 8 PHARMACY WORKS FOR CAREGIVERS

Memory loss and confusion may cause a person to perceive things in new and unusual ways. Caregivers and social workers should understand there will be many unusual changes. Preparation is the key to preventing possibly dangerous behaviors. The preparation involves educating the caregiver with a mountain of information. The pharmacist is the first educator and one of the hardest workers. They have to educate doctors, nurses, psychiatrists, and other health-care workers. They have to know old and new medications. They count pills with great accuracy because it is critical to making a profit and insure a healthy community.

Oddly, robots are slowly taking over the job counting pills and labeling vials. Robots work all day and never complain about eyestrain, doctors' writing, and those nagging-varicose veins. Most government-owned hospitals have two or more robots working for them. The robots use a puff of air to count pills. After eight hours and thousands of puffs, the human brain seizes from the sound of all the miniature explosions. Pharmacists deserve a hefty salary for standing all day, counting pills, and answering a slew of questions from doctors and caregivers. How about "CAREGIVER AWARD" for these guys? Wait a minute for this HERO AWARD!

A pharmacy hires several pharmacy technicians to help the certified pharmacist. A good pharmacist will hire technicians to run the computer and fill the prescriptions. So, what does the certified pharmacist do all day? They run the pharmacy and answer questions about drugs! OK, get awards for all the pharmacy techs! CASE CLOSED!

TIP: Take as many workshops at hospitals and clinics you can. And, don't forget to collect the pamphlets about Alzheimer's. I took pharmacy technology at the local community college before starting my career as a caregiver. I was shocked to see the class full of nurses and caregivers. This class is something most of you don't care to take. The class was time consuming and a background in science and math is highly recommended. The cost was about $2,000 for the semester—it was worth every penny!

However, If you can't pull this off, I would recommend going to a bookstore and buying a pharmacy tech workbook. This workbook covers valuable information about how pills are made, laws concerning drugs, agencies in charge of purity, and measurements used in the pharmacy.

In parts of the country, a pharmacist has the same status as a physician. If your loved one has the flu and a doctor visits your community once a week, ask the pharmacist to "suggest" what would work as a decongestant. If at all possible, keep your loved one out of the waiting room and Senior Centers when flu is rampant. Mom couldn't take the flu shot because she was allergic to eggs. Ask the doctor for the earliest time to take flu shots.

As a caregiver, you are going to have a long relationship with a pharmacist and the pharmacy. Don't be afraid to ask a question about how to cut pills, a missing dosage, or taking pills with or without food. A pharmacist is one of the most brilliant professionals you will ever meet as a caregiver. No appointment needed, just call and ask! It is not uncommon for an elderly patient to have a prescription for six or more drugs. Relax, that number shouldn't bother you because we are living in a modern world. Modern medicine often produces miracles because they are highly tested and regulated.

Machines stir the ingredients for complete mixing of the medication and another machine stamps the pills at lightning speed. If your loved one has ten pills to take each day, don't worry about the number, but instruct them to take one at a time until they are taken. Encourage them to drink some water before they begin taking pills. Act like a cheer leader, because ten pills are hard to take even for healthy people!

Medications are tracked for purity and are highly reliable. The pharmacist's telephone number is on the medicine bottle if problems arise. Your questions can most likely be answered by the pharmacist—not the pharmacy tech. Only certified pharmacists are allowed to answer drug questions. The pharmacist can answer any question about medication and doctors consult them when they have questions.

TIP: Make sure the pharmacy is close to home. Also, make sure the pharmacy has branches and "call in" prescription technology. This is a phone-based ordering by prescription number. The system is vital when you have several prescriptions to order. Call the prescription number and the computer responds to your reply—it has been filled and ready for pick up!

You are going to spend a lot of time in a pharmacy, so make it a convenient place to order and pick up medications. Some people like the convenience of a drive-up when the weather is a problem.

TIP: Change your pharmacy if you don't like the one you selected. If you need a drive up and it doesn't have one, make the change! It takes minutes to change your information sheet to a new pharmacy computer.

Ask your doctor about any of my tips in this book. If he/she disagrees, go with the doctor. If your loved one is taking Chopped-Egyptian Sage or Roasted-Cannia Nuts from Brazil, ask the pharmacist or doctor about the safety of "natural cures" with prescription medications. A lot of accidental poisoning can be prevented by asking the doctor or pharmacist if supplements can be taken with your prescription medications.

I had a terrible time weaning mom off "natural cures" from neighbors. For about a month, neighbors were giving her sport drinks, soda, and some bottled water from a Pacific Island for her abdominal discomfort. Finally, I ask the neighbors not to give her "natural" cures. We didn't consider soda a natural cure with so much sugar. Finally, I called the doctor and he agreed. He said, "Buy the drug for dyspepsia that is an over-the-counter medication to reduce acid and pressure." He gave the trade name and the generic name. The "trade name" was given by the drug company that initially produced the drug. The generic name was given by another company producing the drug after the patent expired.

I told mom the doctor recommended this new medication for your acid reflux. I mentioned it won a Nobel Prize in medicine and was "naturally" found in the sundry section of Wal-Mart. She loves Wal-Mart and didn't question my "natural" statement or the store's staff. The medicine worked in less than 30-minutes. However, mom gave the can of soda credit for relieving her pain and discomfort. Yes, that's Ms. Dollie! She wanted her friends, who brought the soda, to get credit for curing her pain and suffering. We laughed about soda and its sugar as a natural medication for acid reflux.

I often dream of a day when community colleges develop a pharmacy class for caregivers. I think it could be free to the public, but we would have to ask a drug company to host the class. A college could pay pharmacy techs., the person who fills your medicine at the pharmacy, to host the class and explain some things about medication, rules, and guidelines in a pharmacy. TIP: A good pharmacist hires several pharmacy techs to do the counting, filling, and labeling vials. They are identified as techs and without them, a busy pharmacy would grind to a halt. A Pharmacist's primary job is to teach co-workers how to run a modern pharmacy and make a profit. Let's give a "CAREGIVER AWARD" to everybody who works at a pharmacy? Health-insurance companies could host classes on medication during their monthly seminars for the elderly.

I would recommend all caregivers read a few books about nursing before beginning your career. Go to the library or bookstore to the section on nursing and medication. I read several books that had chapters on: Giving medications, medicine and diseases, and caregivers using preventive care.

TIP: One of my favorite books for caregivers was a paperback book on types of heart medicine and how they were used and classified. When your loved one is taking a nap, read a nursing chapter or go on the Internet. Ask your doctor about the validity of Internet topics and questions.

CH. 9 BAD LAWS AND BAD HABITS

Mom developed a bad habit before the first ER trip: She would eat a bite of her meal and place the rest in the frig to eat later. That later could be a week from now. On one frig "clean out," I threw away ten dishes of meals that accumulated in about one week. The doctor knew about her eating habits and prescribed a pill to increase her appetite. I never noticed an increase in food consumption and the doctor soon cancelled the medication after a month. I have heard from caregivers this pill was commonly prescribed to Alzheimer's patients to maintain weight.

I had to watch the expired-food labels like a hawk! Mom would eat things that had already expired. In one situation, a bottle of salad dressing had expired over a year ago. She saw the salad dressing in the trash and placed it back on the frig shelf over and over. I changed cleaning time to the first day of each month. The caps were removed from food expiring that month and thrown away. Some food had to be wasted to prevent another trip to the ER. Expiring foods that month were dumped into the trash; lids were placed into a different trash can. Frozen foods got the same treatment. They were labeled the day of purchase. I used a permanent marker and marked everything before placing it in the freezer. I gave everything frozen one year from the purchase date.

These plans worked well and the threat of food poisoning ended as fast as it started. After living with Alzheimer's most of his life, grandpa actually died from food poisoning. He always had a problem leaving meals on the kitchen counter. His younger wife warned him about the dangers of bacteria, but it was hopeless at his age! He lived at home and his wife took care of him until his death at 97. She told me it never crossed her mind to place him in a nursing home. She said, "I loved him too much to put him in an institution." Caregivers can extend the life of the elderly, but they must have curiosity, training, and lots of love. State laws and strangers must not hinder our efforts to help our loved ones.

In the future, states must take enormous care when passing laws. Bad laws do damage and curb the work of caregivers. Strangers should be asked to avoid the temptation of helping dementia patients without Power of Attorney, Guardianship, and caregiver permission. This protection is required in some states.

Undocumented caregivers have a role in helping families at the present time.Our duties demand help from several caregivers. If your finances allow, hire several caregivers for different times of the day. Undocumented caregivers are another unfortunate situation that needs to be addressed. We can't wait long since the disease has no cure. These caregivers have to be used to help mom/dad live longer and better lives.

Alzheimer's is an unusual disease that has no cure and few treatments. This uniqueness attracts more caregivers than most diseases. For that reason, family members don't fear volunteering for the job. Some family members rotate the job every few years. A caregiver can arrive at 6:00 a.m. and leave at noon. Another can arrive at noon and leave at 6:00 p.m. State laws should recognize the disease for what it takes to keep patients strong and fashion laws for the family.

A neighbor of ours is ninety two years old and is financially able to hire several caregivers. She hires two a day to come to her house and take care of her! She hires only from her church. Her family lives in North Carolina and can't help with hiring caregivers. Her husband passed away years ago, and she is "on her own!" She tells everybody it's not a problem at my age and I like the extra company! She puts a sign on the church- bulletin board. She hires them to come for five days a week and pays slightly over minimum wage. Teens wanting to become nurses crave this part-time work and can study after Jerri goes to sleep. Jerri says, "I enjoy their help because this place is always a mess— I need four caregivers but can't afford them!"

Mom developed a problem concerning her house. She would become anxious and upset over the house. In order for her to vent her anger, she would threatened family and friends about her decision to sell the house. Mom's over-reactive nature with her house, seemed to be a form of control over family and friends. Family members thought it was a cry for attention. On one occasion, she wanted to sell her house and move to Houston to live near her youngest daughter.

I ask her to call and have a discussion with her daughter about such a drastic move. Evidently, she hadn't worked out all the details, because mom couldn't find a place for the dogs to live. And, what about all of your phone buddies, neighbors, friends, and sister who calls you daily? We asked mom, "Will your friends and relatives be able to come and visit in Houston?" She simmered down and forgot the idea. The house was something she always controlled, but her dementia was preventing "full use" of the house. Extra rooms caused consternation because they were empty most of the time. Severe storms worried her about needing a new roof often.

Her home had become a constant anxiety for the last two years. The move to Houston was bantered often, but I believe the distance was too great and her friends objected. She never could find a place to live in Houston, and dropped the idea. On one occasion, mom got so mad living in her house with all those problems, her anger spilled into a yelling event. She said, "I am going to give this house to the next person walking down the road!" I thought for a minute about something to say that would distract her attention. I questioned, "Where would Sarah and Daisy live? They love you and this house so much!" You know how they would feel if they were separated!"

She immediately calmed down and dropped the idea of giving the house away. The house was her last dominion in life. It was in her name and she tried to control things in her life using possessions. Mom tried to control her family, but not her friends. She was always careful not to say or do anything that would upset her friends. A psychologist thought this could be behavior related to her dad's long-held secret. He never wanted his family or relatives talking to strangers or friends about the "family secret."

Unfortunately, Mom's sister has an extra twenty-miles to drive simply because strangers took the wrong approach. ADULT CARE, INC. attempted to help an Alzheimer's patient when there was no reason—she had three-adult kids and a handful of doctors assisting every move she made.

There has to be something inherently wrong with the ADULT CARE, INC. program. These people didn't bother to call or ask if I had a nursing home picked out for mom! These strangers needed to know more about mom's "health history" to make a good decision about her future!

We never thought mom could be placed in a home of any kind for more than a year! Strangers just didn't care and continued searching for an assisted- living home for her. During this time, ADULT CARE, INC. didn't know mom had been released from a Behavioral Hospital seven days earlier under strict guidelines and supervision. Furthermore, I had an attorney preparing a guardianship decree. All of this work was a waste of time and money. ADULT CARE, INC. was working under the P.O. they requested from the court. My attorney dropped my pursuit of guardianship once the judge extended the PO for three months. The judge reiterated: "if nothing happens, it will be dropped." The first judge violated my civil rights and a second judge was protecting the advocates. I felt it was time to file complaints at the state capitol against both judges and ADULT CARE, INC. I always complained locally and then statewide to cover all the tracks.

"The Protective Order shouldn't have been written without some detective work," was a common statement by civil-rights employees. Family and friends asked, "Did the judge ever comment on the way the PO was written. I replied, "No, the laws for PO's seem to be what ADULT CARE believes at a given time. If they don't know a patient has dementia, no one seems to care and the patient is treated as normal. Mom had problems living in a controlled unit at the hospital. Why would our family want her placed into an assisted-living home when her hospital says she can't live alone. Her doctor knew she had dementia, but mom faked illness often and none of the family took her seriously. My two sisters and I worried mom wouldn't be happy in any type of nursing home! Some worried about what had occurred in the behavioral hospital and doubted mom could ever be placed! Let's wait to make these decisions when mom is in Stage 5 or 6?

We did agree she should be close to her sister for anything she needed. The growing town that ADULT CARE, INC. placed mom could present problems for her sister in the future. I tried to help mom's sister understand that mom's present nursing home, could be engulfed by a metropolis in less than five years. That was the primary reason for our interest in placing mom in a nursing home closer to her sister's home in the country. Both of mom's daughters live in Texas and are unable to visit mom as often as her sister. However, mom's sister insisted that we place mom as close as possible to her home. I worried that her sister's health, age, and family commitments prevented a long trip each week and that could end abruptly.

The immediate family knew mom's capability for manipulating the hospital staff and the psychiatrist during the recent hospital stay. If an eighty-five- year-old woman can pull the "wool over the eyes" of the staff at a certified-behavioral hospital, a nursing home would be a calamity! Placing mom into any type of home was going to be a major undertaking for our family. We had no idea that strangers would take over the job for us!

Also, we had no idea strangers would race in and place mom without notifying her doctors at the Behavioral Hospital or any family member. These strangers were ADULT CARE, INC. and Judy, our neighbor.

TIP: Caregivers not only have to watch grandma, but they have to watch their neighbors who can derail well-designed plans for grandma!

After all that has happened to me as a caregiver, I still can't believe my state allows caregivers to be treated with disrespect and contempt. This state has bad laws. Guess what happens to states forcing its citizens to live with bad laws? The answer is: Caregivers file complaints, books are written about awful laws and conditions, and caregivers pray that the state changes its governors and local leaders. Bad laws create jobs for certain careers at the same time reducing the number of caregivers. Bad laws have a tendency to treat families and caregivers poorly. Finally, the quality of life for all citizens will suffer and costs rises for these services. Eventually, the state <u>never</u> makes: TOP TEN BEST PLACES TO LIVE!

Locally, how can an ambulance driver take mom to a hospital that didn't know she was a dementia patient at another? I specifically told the driver to take mom to a certain hospital. How can ambulance services refuse to do their job and get away with negligence? The Fire Chief and I discussed the matter for over an hour without resolve. I told the Fire Chief you guys took mom to the hospital I requested three nights before without hesitation. What has changed in the last three days at the fire department?

He had no answer for this caregiver. If a family requests an ambulance go to a certain location because of an <u>Adult-Safety Plan,</u> why can that request be honored? If the hospital is far away, turn on the lights and siren and step on it!

Any EMT in the country could diagnose mom was faking a "stroke" as she "walked" to the ambulance. This caregiver gave the ambulance staff a hint mom was faking the stroke. There was no hurry going to the ER because mom faked strokes and nausea all the time. This same ambulance team witnessed mom's handy work just three nights earlier. Mom's mother faked illnesses for attention and she must have learned the technique from her.

Finally, we learned about a doctor in a nearby town questioning the same ambulance service. The doctor says mom couldn't be treat for a stroke at that hospital and eventually transferred to another hospital. I guess that is why small towns have what is known as "Growing Pains!" If a mayor and city manager are strong, regulations will change slowly so as not to interfere with the "quality of life" issue! Moreover, you have to have strong leaders at every position or nothing gets done and mistakes are assured! Eventually, if the ambulance and mayor aren't professional, your town never makes: BEST PLACES TO LIVE IN THIS STATE.

I suggest a necklace to prevent such mistakes in the future? A necklace like a "diabetic chain" could relieve caregiver stress. A tag could be worn by all dementia patients for quick ID. I believe a necklace with a fat-red "D" embossed on it from the hospital that diagnosed dementia would work. I don't think the tag would offend anyone if it had a few diamonds on its face. Also, the last four digits of the SSN could help ID the patient.

The Alzheimer's Association offers services to help ensure safety. Medic Alert® + Alzheimer's Association Safe Return® is a 24-houremergency response service that provides assistance when a person with dementia becomes lost or has a medical emergency. Another great service is Alzheimer's Association Comfort Zone®, a comprehensive Web-based location management system that allows families to monitor a person with Alzheimer's. Visit alz.org/safety to learn more about these safety plans.

Mom was transferred from an ER without her caregiver or kids being notified. This is a situation with disaster written all over it! IS THERE A PROFESSIONAL IN THE HOSPITAL? I had no idea medical personnel like doctors, social workers, nurses, and EMT's would treat an eighty-five-year-old woman without reviewing some health records. Mom is eighty five years old—she has a bushel-basket full of records, somewhere! It sounds as if we are living in a third-world country. Evidently, the new ER believed mom's "danger" story and notified the local Sheriff. The Deputy called ADULT CARE, INC. and drove mom to their safe house after 8 p.m. The next day, mom dictated her complaints to DD at CARE SERVICES.

However, mom spent the night in their safe house and she wasn't a "happy camper!" Her room had no heat and she didn't sleep that night. She complained for months about a frozen left foot from sleeping in a safe house without heat and air. My first visit with mom, after the PO expired, turned into a complaint session about no sensation in her left foot.

She was visibly upset with both ADULT CARE, INC. and CARE SERVICES for all the mistreatment while she lived with them. Actually, my first visit occurred almost four months after the officer dropped her off at ADULT CARE, INC. Mother wouldn't sit down and visit, she was anxious, agitated about her foot, talked incessantly to the director of the home, and complained about being an old woman and not having any help. She really didn't know me since it had been over four months since I saw her last. I couldn't communicate with her so I somberly walked her to the hallway and hugged her and said, "Good-bye!"

I visited with the officer's boss and he said his officer "erred on the side of caution." I told the Captain, "No one knows what that statement means!" It is subjective for each officer using the saying. My e-mail to the officer showed he knew mom was in the Behavioral Hospital less than a week before he took mom to ADULT CARE, INC. This officer moved mom without reporting it to her caregiver at 8 p.m. when he was asking for her medications. I told the Captain that his officer "didn't" use "erring on the side of caution" properly or he would have driven mom to her Behavioral Hospital that night for further treatment.

Mom was having delusions and hallucinations when she was taken to the safe house that night. Delusions involve false beliefs and hallucinations are false perceptions of objects or events that are sensory in nature. When an Alzheimer's patient has a hallucination, they see, hear, smell, taste or even feel something that isn't really there. The peeping Tom is a good example of mom's recent hallucination. I don't believe mom ever got over the "Peeping Tom" incident or the alleged theft at the hospital.

I could see Mom in situations where she could see and feel things that weren't present. The man who peeped into her windows at night was real. She could hear, see, and feel him watching her as she watched TV. At night, she often mentioned him having a son who also watched her read books at bedtime. I wanted to ask mom about the "Peeping Tom" looking into her window while she was sleeping. I never questioned her again about the man for fear it would produce anxiety and wandering.

Paranoia is a type of delusion in which a person may believe—without reason—that others are mean, lying, unfair, or out to get them.

Accusations that someone is poisoning their food or medicine, stealing their money, and her caregiver is an imposter are all delusional statements. Stealing money from an Alzheimer's patient is bad enough, but people with Alzheimer's may become suspicious, fearful, or jealous of people. The one statement that hurts caregivers the most: My caregiver isn't who she says she is. Delusions can appear all of a sudden and are symptoms of the disease. Don't hesitate to explain that the person acting this way has Alzheimer's disease!

As a caregiver, please help others understand changing behaviors. Always pass reliable information to other caregivers. Use Websites that have a good reputation for credible-Alzheimer's information. TIP: Make sure family members and other caregivers understand that suspicions and false accusations are caused by the disease. The accusations are not a reflection of the patient. My mother didn't accused me of abusing her, it was the disease. To this day, I still don't know what I was accused of doing!

I could see a lack of interest by the court with the issue of my protective order. The PO was definitely a "shotgun" approach to this disease. My complaints got to offices at the state capitol, and several made personal comments on their letters: "This Protective Order shouldn't have been issued by ADULT CARE, INC.," says a civil rights' advocate. The judge violated your civil rights was another statement often repeated in letters from advocates at the state capitol.

Will the courts have to hire more judges, attorneys, and social workers? If just one in five caregivers is summoned to appear in court, millions of court appearances will be necessary to solve Alzheimer's-related problems in the future. Laws need to be changed in favor of caregivers.

We shouldn't burden the courts with questions about this disease. The disease is bad enough without judges and police involvement. Caregivers know how Alzheimer's patients act and we have to educate the public about the behavior. We must register caregivers at the state level to protect their rights. Otherwise, strangers will take advantage of caregivers.

According to the Alzheimer's Association, more than 5 million Americans have Alzheimer's disease, which is the most common form of dementia accounting for 60 to 80 percent of all cases. This disease also impacts more than 15 million family members, friends, and caregivers.[10]

CH. 10 FROM CLINIC TO BIG CHAIR

Mom's insurance finally paid the bills for her first three trips to the ER. These bills came from the hospital that had difficulty billing patients. I was glad to see the pile of bills disappear. Each "fake-stroke" visit was billed at $3,000. Caregiver's need to develop a good relationship with the supplemental-insurance companies. These insurance companies have a large staff of employees that can help caregivers with many of the day-to-day problems. Explain your situation and ask for help. I filed a complaint with mom's health insurance and they seemed very upset and took my side. "The ER should have called you about your mother's health," they said in a letter to me! They couldn't investigate my case because I didn't have Power.

Mom's insurance company knew each hospital she used for her aches and pains. Many supplemental-insurance companies send preventive medicine in a monthly newsletter: Health and wellness prevention information. These letters direct "social events" for their health-plan members. They welcome friends, grandkids, and caregivers to the Senior Care Center. A sample schedule for Aug: Defensive Driving, Chair Exercise Classes, Movie Day, Estate Planning, and Retirement Living. This is a good way to help mom/dad meet people and have a good time. Most schedule these events during the day and near your loved one's residence.

Mom was totally against nursing homes, but a short stay at the hospital was something she could handle once in a while. I could see mom's attitude change about wandering-by-ambulance. Wandering-by-ambulance was turning into an exciting thing— a vacation once a week. If I couldn't figure out a way to stop her, PO's may be a common thing. Strangers would take over my job and mom would suffer from their inexperience!

I made a promise when I moved in with her four years ago: I would never place her into a nursing home as long as I was in good health and she never moved "into Stage-6" of the disease. At the time I made the promise, we thought mom could never be placed in a nursing home. That horrible week she experienced at the Behavioral Hospital was something we didn't want repeated. Stage-4 Alzheimer's can last up to four years and that was my goal for mother. In approximately five years from now, I would ask the doctor to let me know when she was in Stage-5 and I would place her in the nursing home close to her sister's house. Caregivers must set some goals with their loved ones. Your ability to take care of him/her is limited in Stage-6 and waiting that long to institutionalize him/her could be a bad move. Most moves into a assisted-living homes are done around Stage 5 or 6. Mom's personality was one that wanted control by manipulation. Her personality was one of confrontation until she got her way. I know it must have driven my two dads crazy living with a wife that used confrontation. One doctor questioned almost everything mom did while she was his patient. The psychiatrist that worked at the Behavioral Hospital was never impressed by mom's behavior. Also, she wasn't used to a doctor telling her to do things she didn't want to do! She disliked everything he said and was confrontational with him. I could see the "confrontational side" of mom and knew it was something a husband would detest after a few years of marriage!

This doctor had the nerve to toss mom from his office. "No one throws Ms. Dollie out of an office," she remarked. Yes, he was the only doctor in mom's life that could figure out her behavior and personality. Her behavior changed during that short time and she used an aggressive tone with her new doctor.

The training and skill this doctor must have had to figure out Ms. Dollie! She would turn off a doctor if they said something she didn't like or approve. I listened to the doctor's conversation with mom and she didn't have a chance with this guy. He was a brilliant man and knew mom inside and out! She finally gave up trying to manipulate this professional and started crying incessantly. Crying was mom's backup for what she calls being abused by the doctor.

At office visits, he would inquire why mom hadn't walked more since she lived in the suburbs. He would counter her negative answers by saying, "Now Ms. Dollie, I see no reason in your file you can't walk around your house a few times each day! She would counter, "I can't walk!" He countered, "How did you get to my office?" The doctor would eventually win the "counters" but he didn't know Ms. Dollie was determined to remain in her "BIG CHAIR" for the rest of her life! Mom had told friends and family she couldn't walk. She evidently didn't think now would be a good time to rescind that lie! She hated her new doctor and wanted a new one!

Mom's friends couldn't walk, so after mom's ear surgery she decided she couldn't walk! After telling everybody she couldn't walk anymore because the ear surgery caused her walk to be unstable, they stopped visiting. Mom's story backfired and it made her depressed and lonely. Loneliness crept into her life after ear surgery and stayed until she developed early-stage Alzheimer's.

It had been a bold pledge, but I had to calm her down when she had concerns about nursing homes. Making a promise is a bold thing to do under stress, but they have to be made in a calm manner to Alzheimer's patients. Promises, followed by hugs are done in a manner that calms and settles anxiety. She and I hated the thought of placing her into a nursing home or assisted-living unit. She worried for days about the possibility.

The ER doctor at the first emergency-room visit, over six months ago, told me it was most likely food poisoning and not high-blood pressure they were investigating. The ER doctor emphasized: "Your mother is in excellent- physical health for someone her age," The doctor did a prognosis for our family: "After reviewing all of her numbers, he believed she could live to 102." The ER doctor continues, "She told me her mother lived into her 90s and her dad almost 100, so it is very possible for your mother to achieve that age." I asked the doctor, "What are you trying to say?"

He replied quickly, "She could outlive her kids and you need to think about a nursing home with a mental capacity." This ER doctor was a former college classmate of mine and was first to discuss a nursing home with a "mental section." My mother hadn't been evaluated with "dementia or psychosis" at this point and it startled me. It would be another two years before asking for an evaluation following a wandering event.

The next day, we found a nursing home in a small town near her sister's home. That nursing home was the only facility that was near her sister and adapted for "mental." The director assured me they had a good reputation and wanted mom to visit soon. My fishing buddy's mother was placed in this home and they were happy with the staff and location for his mother. I made an appointment to take mom for a visit the following Tuesday.

However, it was all in vain; ADULT CARE, INC. placed Mom in a nursing home far from her sister's house. Judy, our neighbor, helped ADULT CARE, INC. move mom to this new assisted living location. Neither Judy nor ADULT CARE, INC. had any idea that she had treatment at the Behavioral Hospital and was considered a patient that could harm herself.Also, neither had any idea that the hospital dismissed mom by agreement she couldn't live by herself. I was upset that Judy was a type of person that didn't bother to call about recent changes in mom's health. I saw a part of Judy that none of us had ever seen before and we didn't like her meddling into family matters. Judy is a good example of strangers doing Alzheimer's.

CH. 11 "LACK-OF-DISEASE"

In summary, I took mom to the ER, by car, three times during the winter. On two occasions in March, she traveled by ambulance for a total of five ER trips by early spring. For some reason, mom discovered it was more exciting to wander-by-ambulance—just push a button and she was off to the "races." If her stories convinced an ER staff, she would spend the night in the hospital away from "Peeping Tom" and those dangerous teenagers flooding her front yard.

At the hospital, she would receive lots of attention, greet strangers, talk to nurses, and have a team of doctors to manipulate. Mom preferred the atmosphere of a hospital over sleepless nights with her dogs. An Osteopathic doctor suggested mom's sleeping habits were wrecking her diet, mood, physical stamina, and behavior. He ask her to get out of the "Big Chair" and walk around the house several times a day.

It had slipped my mind to mention "Peeping Tom" walked that same route. Mom would hesitate exercising in that area for fear of running into him. But, she wasn't going to exercise or walk around the house for any health benefits! Mom's life turned sedentary when she reached thirty years old. I believe the thyroid surgery gave her depression because it was cancerous. The surgeon was a friend of the family and said, "This is a common cancer and you shouldn't worry about it spreading—I got all of it!"

Mom's three kids and two husbands hopelessly tried to change her sleeping habits. I wanted the anxiety and depression pills to continue. I thought we could see less napping when she was taking the depression meds. Mom's sleep patterns were ruining her health and the "Big Chair" wasn't helping the situation. Her sleeping habits became unorganized and she used the Big Chair as a bed for naps. Friends suggested she was depressed before the diagnosis of dementia and psychosis. And, to make things worse, she started a long process of self-medication and fought doctors about the need for such medication. Mom asked me, "Should

I be taking depression medication when I am not depressed?" I replied, "Try it and see if it makes a difference in your energy and your sleeping habits."

Her doctor reminded the family to keep her mentally active and walk as much as possible. It was much better to be in a hospital when she felt lonely. Like many people her age, loneliness is a major problem with or without dementia. She told me on several occasions she was lonely most of the time. I asked, "Would you like for me to drive you to your sister's house twice a week?" I have to go by her house on the way to the fishing hole. It wouldn't be a problem to drop you off on the way and pick you up on the way back. Mom's sedentary lifestyle always had a standard reply for travel, "No, I can't ride that far!"

What would you say if I would dropped you off at the Senior Citizen's Center on Fridays instead of going to the lake? She said, "No, those people are too old for me! I don't' want to change Friday because the dogs have so much fun swimming and chasing ducks and geese. She reminded me, "I don't like being around old people!" I added, "Mom, you're eighty five years old, there has to be someone younger at the Center."

She replied, "No, I don't want to go to the Center by myself." If you will call your best friend, I'll pick her up every Thursday morning and take you guys to the Center. Call when you are tired and I'll pick you up. She refused to go to the center because the "Big Chair" was part of her life—she ate meals, napped, played with the dogs, and watched TV in the "Big Chair." Her dogs had the same lifestyle and became sluggish and overweight. Vet orders came down quickly: "I want you guys to walk these dogs daily until they lose weight!"

Mom's five ER visits over a period of six months were upsetting her. The doctors weren't cooperating due to insurance rules and guidelines. Her Supplemental-insurance company suggested she exercise with them. It is common for lonely-senior citizens to abuse hospital stays for a variety of emotional problems. Mom's friends were going to the hospital regularly. They would ask if she had been hospitalized lately. Of course, mom didn't want to be left out going to a hospital, so she worried something was wrong. Her trips to the p-c doctor didn't satisfy these "needs." She always wanted her friends visit her in the hospital. But, her excellent-physical health prevented that wish from coming true. Her friends would talk about their latest surgery and how long they had to stay in the hospital. I knew mom was experiencing sadness related to a "lack-of-disease."

Mom's efforts to be admitted to any hospital were flawed because her friends lived far away and none could drive a car. Furthermore, they would have to call to visit her in the hospital. We thought that could be mom's recent motivation to go to the hospital—it would produce lots of "attention." The attention and phone calls from friends were likely the reward mom was seeking. I wish I could cure loneliness and Alzheimer's with one pill!

CH. 12 ALZHEIMER'S GUIDE TO STAGES

<u>STAGE 1: Normal outward behavior</u>

The person does not experience any memory problems. In this early phase, he won't have any symptoms that you can spot.

<u>STAGE 2: very mild changes</u>

You still might not notice anything in their behavior, but he may be picking up on small differences, things that even a doctor doesn't catch. This could include forgetting a word or misplacing objects. At this stage, subtle symptoms of Alzheimer's don't interfere with his ability to work or live independently. Keep in mind that these symptoms might not be Alzheimer's at all, but simply normal changes from aging. These and other studies offer hope that someday we may have tools that could help detect Alzheimer's early, track the course of the disease, and monitor response to treatments.

<u>STAGE 3: Mild Cognitive Decline</u> (Early-stage Alzheimer's may be diagnosed in some, but not all, individuals at this point).

It is at this point that you start to notice changes in their thinking and reasoning.

Examples:

1) Forgets something he just read
2) Asks the same question over and over
3) Has more and more trouble making plans or organizing
4) Can't remember names when meeting new people

You can help by making sure he pays his bills and gets to appointments on time. You can also suggest he ease stress by retiring from work and putting his legal and financial affairs in order.

KEY TERMS (SYMPTOMS)
_____

Cognitive: Symptoms that affect memory, awareness, language, judgment, and ability to plan, organize and carry out other thought processes.

Behavioral: A group of additional symptoms that occur to at least some degree in many individuals with Alzheimer's. In early stages, people may experience personality changes such as irritability, anxiety or depression.

In later stages, individuals may develop sleep disturbances; wandering impulses; agitation (physical and verbal aggression, general emotional distress, restlessness, pacing, shredding paper or tissues, yelling); delusions (firmly held belief in things that are not real); or hallucinations (seeing, hearing feeling things that are not there).[11]

STAGE 4: Moderate Cognitive Decline (Mild or early-stage Alzheimer's)*

During this period, the problems in thinking and reasoning get more obvious.

Examples:

1) Forget details about himself or events.
2) Have trouble putting the right date and amount on a check.
3) Forget what month or season it is.
4) Have trouble cooking meals or even ordering from a menu.
5) Forgetfulness about one's own personal history.
   Becoming moody or withdrawn, especially in socially or mentally challenging situations.
6) Impaired ability to perform challenging mental arithmetic (e.g., counting backward from 100 by 7s)

*People often are diagnosed in this stage.

STAGE 5: Moderately severe cognitive decline (Moderate or mid-stage Alzheimer's) Gaps in memory and thinking are noticeable, and individuals begin to need help with day-to-day activities. At this stage, those with Alzheimer's may:

1) Be unable to recall their own address, phone number, the high school or college they attended.
2) Become confused about where they are or what day it is.
3) Have trouble with less challenging mental arithmetic (e.g., counting backward from 40 by subtracting 4s)
4) Need help choosing proper clothing for the season.
5) Still remember significant details about themselves and their family.
6) Continue to eat or use the toilet unassisted.
7) They may have hallucinations, delusions, and paranoia, and may behave impulsively.

STAGE 6: Severe cognitive decline (Moderately severe or mid-stage Alzheimer's). Memory continues to worsen, personality changes take place and individuals need significant help with daily activities.

The person may:

1) Lose awareness of recent experiences as well as their surroundings.

   Remember their own name but have difficulty with their personal history.

   Distinguish familiar and unfamiliar faces but have trouble remembering the name of a spouse or caregiver.

   Need help dressing properly and may, without supervision, make mistakes such as putting pajamas over daytime clothes or shoes on the wrong feet.

Experience major changes in sleep patterns—sleeping during the day and becoming restless at night.

2) Need help handling details of the toilet.

3) Have increasingly frequent trouble controlling their bladder or bowels.

   Experience major personality and behavioral changes, including suspiciousness and delusions (e.g., believing the caregiver is an imposter) or compulsive, repetitive behavior like hand-wringing or tissue shredding.

4) Be at risk for wandering or becoming lost.

STAGE 7: Very severe cognitive decline (Severe or late-stage Alzheimer's) In the final stage of this disease, individuals lose the ability to respond to the environment, to carry on a conversation, and eventually to control movement. They may still say words or phrases. At this stage, individuals need help with much of their daily personal care, including eating and using the toilet.

They may also lose the ability to smile or sit without support and hold their heads up. Reflexes become abnormal. Muscles grow rigid. Swallowing is impaired.

The seven-stage framework is based on a system developed by Barry Reisberg, M.D., clinical director of the New York University School of Medicine's Silberstein Aging and Dementia Center.[12]

CH. 13 SUNDOWNING

People with dementia and Alzheimer's may have problems sleeping or increases in behavior problems that begin at dusk and last into the night. Mom's five wanderings occurred between dusk and early morning.

Her first wandering was on foot to a neighbor's house 100-yards away. The ground had patches of snow and the temperature was 19° F. The alarm system went off at 3:25 a.m. I thought someone was in the house I got a rifle and walked through the house. The back door of the garage was ajar. I noticed both dogs walking in front of the garage door. Mom had used the garage-door opener to close the door as she walked into the night. The dogs were excited as they waited for me. They waited patiently near the front of the garage door for permission to hunt mom down! I placed the rifle against the door jam and pushed the garage-door opener on the wall. I motioned the dogs: "Sic 'um!" Both raced into the darkness and disappeared. They barked for a time after they disappeared. Daisy, the Shih Tzu, made a ninety-degree turn when she got to the road. I could hear both dogs barking to my "left." Daisy barked for a while and stopped. We live in a suburb and the houses are on 1 ½-acre lots and no fences.

Sarah, the miniature Schnauzer, quickly disappeared into the night barking a regular pattern. My money was on Sarah to find mom first—she has excellent hunting skills. About 100-yards away, there was a house that had lights on the ground looping the front yard. I could see something moving in front of the lights. The lights appeared to go "on and off" as object moved to my right. Sarah's barking seemed to have stopped all of a sudden. I found mom in less than 10-minutes! I knew it had to be mom because her favorite flashlight produced a bluish glow in the dark. I yelled, "Mom, are you out there?" I heard a faint voice, "Yes, I thought I would take a walk in the cool air for a while." I said, "It's winter and the temperature is 19°. You know the flu is going around and you can't take the shot." As I got closer to mom, I asked, "What are you doing this early in the morning?"

She replied, "I couldn't sleep and just wanted to get out of the house for a while." I repeated, "Come back, right now, you and the dogs could get hit by someone going to work." She repeated her recent drama, "You are not going to hurt me are you!" I said, "No one is going to hurt you in this area, we have no crime out here. Everybody likes everybody! Please come back to the house."

By this time, the second alarm had gone off for several minutes and there was a car lighting the road from the west. The second alarm was loud enough to hurt the dogs' ears and they couldn't tolerate it much longer. The dogs refused to come in the house and I worried the slow moving car could be a regular car on the road or the Sheriff. I finally got the alarm turned off and the dogs followed mom indoors. The first wandering-by-foot ended as fast as it started. Mom's recovery occurred so fast the neighbors were unaware she wandered that night.

Nighttime restlessness doesn't last forever. It typically peaks in the middle stages, and then diminishes as the disease progresses. This activity, mostly at night, was ruining our sleeping habits. Mom started sleeping more during the day. It wasn't unusual for her to start napping at 9:30 a.m. and continue to 3:00 p.m.

Chasing mom around at all hours made me sleepy for my fishing trips at 5:30 a.m. Relatives and friends tried to persuade mom not to sleep in the afternoon, but it was a waste of time. I gave her some milk and bananas at 7 p.m. and it seemed to help. Her doctor decided to move her anxiety medicine from 4 p.m. to 5 p.m. and it made a world of difference. However, a week later, mom wandered-by-foot to a neighbor's house at 10:30 p.m.

In the last three months, mom couldn't go through a day without experiencing one of the following behaviors: suspicion, anxiety, or confusion. Finally, one medic asked: Does your mother have dementia? I mentioned to the medic, on the first wandering-by- ambulance: "She was released from the Behavioral Hospital with a diagnosis of dementia with Lewy bodies. Mom told them she had severe pain in her abdomen and get her to an ER right away. It didn't seem to matter how much I mentioned her dementia and Stage-3 Alzheimer's, the EMT's were only concerned with her self-diagnosed nausea. Her doctors and nurses weren't concerned about her wandering and being hit by a car.

The ER doctors guessed she was an Alzheimer's candidate and never thought about calling the police for assistance. Even though mom's stories were comical, the Behavior Hospital staff had enough experience with the elderly they knew they were observing a dementia patient with psychosis.

Mom's stories could get an audience: She told a familiar story about a group of teenagers loitering under the maple tree in her front yard and the Peeing Tom.

"They scare me," she convincingly told the nurses. The nurses laughed without constraint as they discussed teen problems with mom. The nurses were the worst of the bunch—they laughed and were incorrigible.

You couldn't tell it was an Emergency Room by all the laughter and danger stories being passed around. Mom acted like a comedian "working" the small crowd to persuade them to let her spend the night with them. Surely, they wouldn't dare turn her down for a safe place to spend the night after hearing all those "horror stories."

Of course, neither the man nor teens existed, but the ER doctors and nurses seem to find the stories very funny. To calm mom, I told her I would notify the sheriff if the teens returned. Mom's stories spread to our neighbors. One neighbor replied, "I saw the man she is talking about. He was looking into my bathroom window that same night." In disgust, I reminded Alice, "All bathroom windows use a special glass that makes them opaque." I have two people in the dark of night, about the same age, hallucinating together.

I immediately told Alice that mom hallucinated mostly on Friday nights when she saw the Peeping Tom. Alice was the one who helped convince mom to go to the Behavioral Hospital. Perhaps, I should have asked the Intake Coordinator to consider both women for special treatment.

Finally, on the last wandering-by-ambulance at an entirely new hospital, an ER staff did something stupid: After listening to mom's "danger stories," they called the Sheriff in another county. The Sheriff's Deputy took mom to ADULT CARE, INC. in another town for legal action against me. Further, mom was to be taken to her Behavioral Hospital if any incident occurred. What kind of professional staff do we have working in our neighborhood ER's, that call the sheriff on an eighty-five-year-old dementia patients?

Bringing her back was part of her Adult Safety & Self-Care Agreement she had signed less than a week before. Strangely, CARE SERVICES had checked mom's house only three weeks before and they reported mom could harm herself in her own home. Judy had turned mom into Care Services for the investigation of abuse. This stranger, Judy, had no idea about mom's recent hospitalization and a Safety Agreement that she helped mom violate! CARE SERVICES did a sloppy job and thought that would be the end of the matter and closed the case! I was never interviewed by CARE SERVICES.

The officer who helped find mom on two occasions didn't tell ADULT CARE, INC. or CARE SERVICES about mom's wanderings or dementia. I wasn't able to interview the officer, but I did send him two e-mails notifying him of mom's hospitalization in late winter. He knew mom had been released recently from the Behavior Hospital. Why didn't the officer take mom to her hospital? This is a good example of strangers doing Alzheimer's and not caring what happens to the patient or caregiver.

It is becoming harder to rely on the police to do the right thing for dementia patients. Sometimes the best training is not good enough and the officer should be dismissed when bad decisions arise in his/her career. This officer didn't think to tell CARE, INC. that mom was a wanderer. She could have lost her life because of his blunder! This officer has no business working around dementia patients or the public! A possible solution would be to train several officers as "Alzheimer's-Counselors to fill "grave yard and "swing shifts when patients are most likely to wander! What about calling a caregiver before imposing a legal solution?

ADULT CARE, INC. wasn't told by the Deputy that mom was a wanderer. When they found out she was a wanderer, she was treated differently. Mom could have hurt herself or walked away while under their care. The officer knew she was a wanderer because he found her on two occasions. They started placement right away to get mom out of their "hair!" They knew their report was now fraudulent, but what could they do? I notified the Chief, who fished with me, and he said, "ADULT CARE INC. had trouble placing your mother after they discovered she was a wanderer."

I got calls for days from strangers who claimed to have mom in their nursing facility. They asked if I could write a check to cover mom's so- called expenses! Obviously, I didn't write any checks to strangers. After several calls, I replied: "I don't even know where my mother is located and I am not writing checks to strangers! One so-called director wanted $300 for snacks and another $500 to cover blankets and bedding supplies for ten nights. Since I now had a PO on me, the callers would never give me the nursing home's name or location. I was so upset with ADULT CARE, I wrote my State Rep for help and he was given a "snow-job."

Finally, I drove to Judy's place of business and asked her if she helped ADULT CARE, INC. place mom into a nursing facility? Judy proudly admitted, "Yes, I helped ADULT CARE, INC. place your mother in an assisted-care home. I asked, "Why are you involved in this matter?" Her reply was typical for strangers doing Alzheimer's: "You weren't doing anything to keep her safe, so I decided to help!" YES, YOU HEARD IT RIGHT—THIS IS A GREAT STATE BUT NOT FOR ALZHEIMER'S PATIENTS AND CAREGIVERS!

A month later, I discovered mom was in an assisted-living home and her bank statement says so! ADULT CARE, INC. took mom away and a bank statement came in the mail to verify her new address. The statement had mom's new address on a "change-of-address" card. Strangers, without Power of Attorney or Guardianship, got mom's bank statements sent to her nursing home. The bank statement asked if she changed her address and if further changes needed to be made at this time. I was appalled that strangers changed her bank statement without my okay. I called friends and relatives and advised them of mom's new address and phone number. We finally found mom after weeks of calling nursing homes, neighbors, and friends. I was born in this state; the laws are just too crazy for caregivers.

On mom's last trip to the ER, did doctors diagnose mom with severe "suspicion" behavior related to Alzheimer's? The answer is, "No!" because they never had her health records or called the hospital where her records were kept. The ER never called any of her relatives, including me! THIS IS MEDICINE IN THE 21ST CENTURY? Remember, I was at her Behavioral Hospital waiting for mom to arrive by ambulance. On arrival, I was going to ask the ambulance to take her straight to admissions and ask for an intake nurse. I wrote a letter to her supplemental-insurance company and filed a complaint against the Heart Hospital. The insurance company said they would be happy to file a grievance for me, but I would have to have Power of Attorney for my mother! I replied, (part omitted)!

The "stroke" was problematic that night; This case was closed quickly by the ER staff after they called the Sheriff. The Sheriff decided to turn it over to Adult Care, Inc. They filed a PO on me the next day! I wasn't surprised they didn't have any trouble finding me to issue and sign the Protective Order! Instead of referring Mom to her mental health hospital that night, she was taken to a hospital where her records "weren't" kept or shared. "What can go wrong?" What about the records on the ambulance drivers' computer—all phone numbers and medications were supposed to be on the machine. Where did all the data go? What happened to all of her Monday night records and telephone numbers? To any Hospital Staff or ER's in America: Alzheimer's patients are not normal and they need to be treated in a mental-health facility. If you don't have a mental-health doctor at 5:30 p.m., you need to make a call! A News Flash: The country is filling up with eighty-five-year-old mothers. Transferring Alzheimer's patients to places like Adult Care, Inc. for possible legal action ISN'T "ETHICAL TREATMENT" IN THE 21ST CENTURY— SHAME ON ALL OF YOU!

CH. 14 ADULT SAFETY AND SELF-CARE AGREEMENT

Before mother was dismissed from the Behavioral Hospital, her release was contingent on her following a list of rules. The Behavioral Hospital made her sign the agreement: ADULT SAFETY AND SELF-CARE AGREEMENT. The agreement had no standing with mom; she didn't even listen to these rules as the social worker read them. The following is an exact copy of the agreement she signed before dismissal:

I agree to take care of myself and refrain from any behavior which might result in harm to myself or others.

I agree to take the following steps to keep myself and others safe, as well as take care of myself.

1. Son J.P. to monitor safety and coordinate care; son will dispense & monitor meds.
2. Son will make sure house is safe; ie locks installed.
3. Friends are not to tell you how or if to take meds.

I realize that I am responsible for my own actions, and I agree that if I start to feel overwhelmed by the idea of harming myself or others, I will do one of the following

- Contact one or more of the people identified on the plan described above.
- Contact the Hospital at (telephone #) and ask to speak with an Intake Counselor.
- Go directly to the Hospital's Clinical Assessment Department.
- I realize this is open 24 hours a day, 7 days a week.
- Go to the nearest hospital emergency room.

Patient signature and date:

CH. 15 FINAL TRIP TO THE EMERGENCY ROOM

In mid-March, eight days after being released from the Behavioral Hospital, mother casually told me she didn't want her dogs. She asked,"Could you find them a good home?'

It was a warm day and she was in the front yard sitting in her walker. She was sipping water through a straw and getting a little Sun. Dehydration was problematic since winter. I felt something big was about to go down. She cared more for those dogs than anything in the world. I quickly responded, "I will take care of them for you. What are your plans for the day?" I recalled some tips the social worker at the hospital ask me to use to get her mind on something else when such situations occur. The hospital recommended changing her thoughts as quickly as possible.

I said, "Let's take a trip to town." She didn't respond, so I knew she planned to wander if the dogs didn't get in the car. A short trip usually did the trick and made her lose track of her thoughts. Today was a different story and she seemed determined to wander earlier than usual—5 p.m. I left briefly to get her car key and check the doors. I was going to make one more attempt because Daisy was going nuts after she heard me say the word "traveling." Actually, both dogs responded to "let's go traveling" and headed for her car. Both were excited as I opened the back door of the car. Mom would be more likely to take a trip if the dogs seem excited and in the back seat.

At 5:10 p.m., she push her LifeBand button because I could hear it go off as I passed the speaker in the house. Mom was talking to the operator on her portable phone—she needed an ambulance for some reason. As I entered the garage, the operator's questions were directed to fire or police. My mother was repeating, "I think I am having a stroke and rush one real quick!" Mom was standing outside the garage when she was giving all of these instructions to LifeBand. She was talking on the phone with the operator when I mentioned, "I have the keys, let's go traveling!"

Both dogs jumped into the back seat and seemed excited about traveling. My goal was to get mom in the front seat to prevent her from wandering. If mom planned to wander to a hospital, I would have to notify them because it would be a violation of her Safety Agreement. I didn't want to take the dogs to the Behavioral Hospital so I was carefully monitoring the situation.

She would be admitted for further treatment at the Behavioral Hospital tonight. Mom didn't know what she was doing because it meant at least two weeks in the ward she just left a few days ago. It would cause embarrassment to see her old friends betting on her return.

I shouted to the operator at LifeBand, "She's not allowed to go to just any Hospital. Mom just got out of the Behavioral Hospital last week for dementia." She is still a patient at that Behavioral Hospital!" I knew it was a waste of time talking to the operator before the ambulance arrived. It would be safer in an ambulance than walking the streets in the dark. I replied to the operator, "Go ahead and send an ambulance—I will tell them what they need to know when they arrive, Thank you!"

I looked at Mom and said, "I promised to come and get you after calling your sister." She said, "Okay." I watched the scene play out for a second time in four days. None of us had the slightest idea this wandering would be the last for mom and me. We never dreamed two neighbors would take over mom's care before I could get her back to the Behavioral Hospital for treatment.

This is a good example of strangers interfering with caregivers. Several caregivers followed my plight with mom's neighbors. One caregiver told me that her mother was treated for a month at the same hospital and she is doing well after that length of time. Her opinion was similar to mine— it must take a month to help Alzheimer's patients work through their problems and medications.

All the Deputy had to do was remind the ER staff of her release from the Behavioral Hospital. By not informing the ER she had dementia and was a patient at another hospital, they had no choice in the matter. Also, her p-c doctor would never okay she be taken to ADULT CARE, INC. for legal dispensation and then admitted to a nursing home in Stage 3 Alzheimer's! This outrageous activity was criminal and is an example of strangers doing Alzheimer's and doing it badly! The strangers in this event were: Fire department, Judy, Alice, Deputy, and the Heart Hospital's ER staff.

Caregivers have to be on your toes working with these people or my case may come to your neighborhood. We worried who would be taking care of her for the next three months. I called my attorney about our dogs. Five days after the summons, CARE SERVICES was trying to find a key to our house to water and feed the dogs. This is animal cruelty and CARE SERVICES and ADULT CARE, INC. should have been prosecuted. I drove to the local newspaper and complained to them about mom and the dogs' treatment. The paper did nothing about such vulgarity.

ADULT CARE, INC. and Judy, our neighbor, placed mom into an assisted-living home that the family did not approve. Our neighbor just took it on her own to slander me about my care to ADULT CARE, INC. I called and wrote letters to State Reps about ADULT CARE, INC. Judy told them mom was scared of J.P. This is a good example of how neighbors, who knew nothing about mom's recent hospitalization, can interfere with a caregiver's job. I complained to my attorney about Judy's careless attitude placing mother without family permission. Most caregivers place family members when they are diagnosed in Stage-5 or 6 —never in Stage 3 Alzheimer's!

Also, I took a trip to her doctor's office to ask why her medications were revoked—she was taking only thyroid and eye drops in court records. He had no answer for this caregiver and seemed like a "deer in headlights!" This is a good example of why you should avoid young doctors. He should have demanded ADULT CARE, INC. take mom directly to the Behavioral Hospital for further treatment. This is another example of strangers doing Alzheimer's, but the stranger is a young and inexperience doctor!

What kind of charge would the court make on a caregiver with no criminal history? How could a court believe an Alzheimer's patient that was incoherent, delusional, and hallucinating that night in the ER? Wandering- by-ambulance is just as dangerous as wandering-on-foot for the patient and caregiver. The hospital reported caregiver abuse to the Sheriff without proof and from our neighbor who knows nothing about Alzheimer's patients!

This last wandering started in the late afternoon and mom was excited because she thought they were finally admitting her to the hospital. However, later that night, the sheriff took her to another town for abused adults. She was admitted to ADULT CARE, INC. for the next three days. During those three days, there would be no ER staff, no nurses, no family calling about her health or location, and no ADULT CARE STAFF to visit.

Mom acted too sick to be directing the ambulance crews Thursday night. She would get the "stroke plan" ready to pull on the ambulance crew when they arrived. Later at the ER, the staff would get a taste of that "plan" in an effort to spend the night with them. If she had time, mom added "chest pains" and "I'm in danger at home" to her deception to seal the deal. If this repertoire didn't seem to be working, mother added her old favorites:

Peeping Tom and the restless teens under the maple tree. This new hospital wasn't ready for mom's onslaught and acted neglectful and irresponsible. I didn't hesitate to report the new hospital to my State Rep.

We watched mom wander-by-ambulance twice in four days. She always used the same drama: "I am in danger! I am in danger!" But, she forgot to mention that it wasn't from her son, but from the teens loitering in her yard, the man peeping into her windows, and the volume of imaginary people walking through her kitchen. One hospital fell for her ruse: it was the Heart Hospital that used a lockdown at the deputy's request.

The other hospitals had ER crews more experienced and they just laughed and joked with her. They knew her intentions by the way mom acted in their ER.

The Deputy couldn't understand how my mother's disease caused her to act the way she did. Everyone thinks they know Alzheimer's, but they really don't! People, in general, know only about the later stages (6 thru 7) of the disease. That time frame is generally when the disease is ravaging the brain and is physically noticeable. The officer handed mom over to the so- called experts that were actually uneducated advocates. These people took mom's care under false pretense. They had no idea mom was a wanderer because the deputy failed to tell the advocates. The Behavior hospital warned me that she could harm herself in isolated situations like this.

Finally, these same people directed traffic for mom for the next three months. They barely knew mom at this point. These advocates didn't know she had dementia, psychosis, in Stage-3 Alzheimer's, and no health records following her travels. WHAT POSSIBLY COULD GO WRONG?

Perhaps my e-mail was the determining factor to take mom to ADULT CARE, INC. instead of returning her to the Behavioral Hospital. "Erring on the side of caution" would suggest the best and honorable thing to do was to <u>call me</u> or <u>take mom</u> to the Behavioral hospital— the officer did neither! I think the officer was mad at me for an e-mail I sent weeks before this happened. I questioned his honesty and integrity in that e-mail. Further, I had filed a complaint against a fellow officer a few years ago. This officer had lied in a police report during my divorce in a nearby county. My ex- wife's attorney was "permanently disbarred" for asking this officer's to lie in his report. The officer got a slap on the hand for the false report!

During my four years as a caregiver, mom experienced symptoms from the first four stages of Alzheimer's. When new problems occurred, It was never easy for her doctor to surmise what stage she was in at time. Everybody that has Alzheimer's acts and progresses differently because patients are in different stages of the disease! Seven stages of the disease can create quite a range of possible behavior. So, what can you do for the patient? You pass the patient on to someone and hope they can handle the paranoia and delusions. Then, you ask strangers to write a Protective Order for court. This all sounds crazy and irrelevant to me, but it did happen in my county.

Mom was agitated all day after I told her I got an appointment with her primary-care physician earlier that morning. Mom wanted to know when was the appointment? I said, "Monday." It is important that the primary- care doctor see the patient after an emergency-room visit or a wandering event. The doctor may want to admit your loved one to a Behavioral Hospital for further treatment. Since mom wandered the previous Monday night, she was seeing the doctor for at wandering event on the following Monday. I had no idea she was planning another wandering event on Thursday night. Yes, that's Ms. Dollie!

Mom always liked her new p-c doctor because his clinic was a mile from her house, and he would always listen to her problems taking medicine. She was taking six pills and eye drops at night. The number of pills overwhelmed her causing mom to become anxious and suspicious.

On one occasion, she thought I was in collusion with her doctor to get her to take multiple pills. In her mind, she thought the pills were given to make her sick rather to make her well. This is a form of paranoia when mom thinks the doctors are mean to her. For a while, mom thought I was writing prescriptions continuous with the doctor. She was getting headaches and I had to remind her that I am not a doctor. Her doctor provided just what mom needed: sympathy.

Mom had her thyroid removed at thirty years old for cancer. After the surgery, mom lost her sense of smell and taste. We didn't know if it were related to the surgery or dementia. She had a lifetime prescription for one medication after surgery. Throughout life, she took only one pill. However, my step dad asked her to take anxiety and depression medication when she had bouts of stress in her life.

I ask her new primary-care physician if she could cut back on the number of medications because they were overwhelming her. I found pills discarded on the kitchen floor and in trash cans. I placed her breakfast pills in one glass jar, lunch in the second, and dinner in the third. Even though the jars were empty, mom would ask if she had taken the breakfast or lunch pills. Mom's anxiety pills were to be cut in half—half was given at breakfast and the other half at dinner. She spent hours talking to friends who lived throughout the state. None were healthy enough to drive and visit in person. They visited for hours on the phone each day— exchanging medication problems and any new drugs for Alzheimer's.

Her friends persuaded her to stop taking certain medications because some pills were "bad" medicine for them. One friend persuaded mom not to take a certain anxiety medication because she had side effects taking those "green" capsules. At pill taking time, Mom refused to take two different pills because they were considered "BAD PILLS" by her friends. I called the Intake Counselor at the hospital for help. She walked me through "Giving Medication to the Elderly-101." The training was simple: Find someone in the immediate family that could pressure mom to take her pills.

Mom's friends had too much influence on her medication. On four occasions, I had to call her sister and asked for help. It took her sister thirty minutes of congenial counseling for mom to give in and take her meds. Mom acted like a small child taking medication that had a bad taste. Yes, that's Ms. Dollie at 85. Mom and her friends would talk for hours about the side effects of various drugs they were taking. Most of her friends were the same age and had similar health problems. They often complained about a capsule that made them nauseous. We all grew up taking "one" aspirin a day and go to bed. Now the doctor says, "Take "six" pills a day after meals. The shear number of pills quirked her mind. Taking pills caused instant anxiety and forced me to call her doctor and Intake Nurses for help.

Finally, the Intake Counselor suggested some valuable information for the new situation. The Counselor asked if I would call everyone she knew and request that they not discuss her medications. I called the nurse and ask if she could write a form letter. She replied, "No, because the request would sound odd in print."

I mentioned this request to her p-c doctor. Her doctor decided he would change just the pills mom thought was giving her a headache. I know this sounds crazy but it worked! On the next visit, I asked the doctor if he could reduced her medication even farther. I was still finding pills all over the house and in the pockets of her clothing when I washed. Her doctor decided changing brands might work the best. Those "bad pills" suddenly changed color! His suggestion saved time and money looking up addresses of more than twenty friends. The disagreeable "green" capsule turned into a shiny- purple capsules.

The doctor and I wanted "confusion" and that's what we got! Mom lost track of all those colors and never complained again. I couldn't believe the consequences of his action. I overheard mom bragging to her friends, "I made J.P. stop giving me that "green" capsule that gave us headaches! The solution was easy and the young doctor solved the problem with little notoriety! I made it a point to call several caregivers that were following my floundering methods and they were eager to try the same trick on their grandpa.

As I left the p-c doctor's office, he alluded to the fact that he thought my mother lacked the ability to understand "any" of her medications. I nodded, "Yes, you are probably correct because I have heard that speech from several doctors and nurses. Ms Dollie hasn't had to take medication in large numbers until recently. The doctor reiterated that Alzheimer's is a fatal disease and you need to be vigilant for your mother's behavior.

Mom's dad always told his family and friends that taking more than three pills a day would turn a patient into a "junkie." He had attended N.Y. Medical School and mom believed every word he said. She mentioned her dad's opinion to doctors at visits. The doctors replied, "I politely disagree with you father. Modern medications are well tested on people your age and these medications have a history of success!" He then looked at mother with a stern face, "Ms. Dollie, you have to take the medicine like I tell you or they don't work!" Mom followed in her dad's footsteps and his opinion ruled. She began questioning every pill that was prescribed by her doctors and compared these pills with her friends.

Mom's life was made complicated by her family life and personality. She was born at the beginning of the Great Depression. The stress of the Depression was enormous on all who grew up in the thirties. Her dad finally told his immediate family the reason for leaving Tennessee. Mom and her sister were in their twenties when Dave informed the family of his predicament. His dilemma placed undue stress on his family for the next fifty years. Dave told them, "I am tired looking over my shoulder. It was a mistake I made when I was young and Busby's death has haunted me all my life."

I dug a pill out of the Schnauzer's mouth one morning. I saw her in the game room trying to lick something out of her mouth. I examined the pill and it had a tooth impression. I was sure the tooth impression came from Sarah's mouth. I showed the pill to the Vet and told him it was one of mom's depression pills. He said the pill had the ability to kill Sarah. I drove to the Vet's office each time I caught Sarah chewing on a pill. He decided it was time for mom's doctor to recommend therapy for mom because she wasn't taking her medication seriously. The Vet was upset and asked me to contact her physician immediately to save Sarah and Daisy's life.

The doctor reduced her medication to four, but refused to do more. This number is important because someone supervising her, before the court hearing, asked the doctor to take her off all but two medications. I couldn't get authorities to tell me who played a part in getting this done. I thought it was time to file a complaint on her doctor for such carelessness. A caregiver suggested they were trying to prove mom didn't have dementia to skirt possible legal action by me. My friends commented, "That is a cruel and inhumane group of people." I replied, "Yes they are, and if I knew their names, I would file complaints." They couldn't be <u>strangers</u> any longer!

Caregivers must file complaints on strangers that behave this way. Your complaint to their boss will most likely verify these strangers aren't doing their job. Thank God for the computer; eventually, I found every name and address and filed a complaints locally and then at the state level. Your complaint will let their boss take a better "look" at who he/she has hired.

Your complaint could be the one that ends their career! I thought they were supposed to help caregivers so we can do a better job for grandma!

Mom seemed to be more agitated and aggressive about strangers walking through the kitchen. Her aggressive behavior was something that just popped up early in the morning. I needed to call her doctor: "Was it related to Alzheimer's?" I asked the doctor's nurse to call if they thought it was related to Alzheimer's. The Behavioral Hospital cautioned me that she could physically attack me or hurt herself during these frustrating periods? I often called my mother's sister and she persuaded mom to "calm down!" Always ask for help from a close relative or friend. I was told to keep track of the time and what may have caused the agitation in my journal. I wasn't worried about he situation because her sister was excellent at calming mom's occasional hallucinations and delusions.

The Alzheimer's Association recommends the following responses for frustrating situations:

1) Try a relaxing activity like music, taking a walk, or card games.
2) Take a break for yourself.
3) Speak calmly using a calm tone, try to reassure the person.
4) Rule out pain which can cause a person to act aggressively.
5) Ensure safety—make sure you and the person are safe. If the person is unable to calm down, seek assistance from neighbors and friends.
6) Always call 911 in emergency situations.

On mom's last trip to the ER it was about 5 p.m. when she pushed the button on her necklace. I knew her primary-care doctor would still be in his office. Although it was near closing time, I got the doctor's nurse to make an appointment for mom. It was a waste of time because the Deputy took mom directly to ADULT CARE, INC. three hours later and started the "legal" circus!

I could tell Mom was still mad about her appointment with her new psychiatrist at the Behavioral Hospital. Her dismissal didn't change her views about the doctor. It was still bothering her and I could tell she was preoccupied and dreading that next visit. I tried to calm her by explaining the visit was two weeks away and the doctor would welcome you back with open arms! He'll probably ask about your activities since he saw you last.

He'll probably want to know about Sarah and Daisy. "He is really a happy and friendly doctor and I am glad you have him," I reminded her.

Mom never knew how serious her condition and seemed constantly on the defensive if someone brought it up in a conversation. This kind of behavior caused her to question our efforts to get her medication adjusted and seek proper care. Her defensive manner was strong enough to call and tell her neighbors, "J.P. and the Mexican living in the house are trying to hurt me with pills!" I asked mom to stop saying such disgusting things to neighbors and friends. I would call her social worker after hearing her repeat these false statements. I was told to keep reporting the behavior and what to do if it got worse. We had a serious problem that worried the hospital and they repeated warnings: "You need to get Guardianship as soon as possible. She might need weeks of treatment!"

As the ambulance arrived for the second time in four days, she told me she thought it was definitely a stroke. I am not a doctor, but I was a medic in the Army, have a master's degree in biology, and taught biology in college for ten years. I am confident I could determine if someone was having a stroke in front of me. This was not a stroke victim standing in front of me!

Mom was a manipulator most of her life! The ambulance crew saw me laughing when they put her on the gurney. She used the same ruse three days before to wander to the Behavioral Hospital. That Hospital would be hard for mother to manipulate because she had been a patient at their clinic. They already had her records when she arrived at the ER complaining about gas and abdominal pain on Monday.

Our discussion about her psychiatrist that morning pushed her into a "frustrating interaction" that day. Her inability to communicate effectively caused fear, sadness, and anxiety. It was enough to push her over the wandering edge and race to the ER.

I would bet money she was faking it again! The young ambulance driver walked towards me and ask if I was following them? I said, "Yes, but I want you to know my mother is faking her stroke! I asked, "You don't remember her Monday night?" He said, "I was driving Monday night, but don't remember!" I asked the driver what kind of INFO goes in the laptop.

I reiterated, "She faked abdominal pain on Monday afternoon and is picking up where she left off— don't fall for it!" I said loudly. He looked at me in an odd and confusing manner and asked, "What's your name and phone number." I said, "You took all of our INFO on Monday!

"Don't you have all of it in your computer?" He glanced at the computer and replied, "Yes, if we came by three days ago, it will still be in the computer." I replied, "Don't you know because I recognize you as the driver on Monday?" Finally, he said, "Yes, I have her records!" I said, "Great," we have to take her to the Behavior Hospital because she needs to be admitted for abusing ER's.

They loaded her into the ambulance for a second time in four days. I gave them a sheet with all of her drugs plus eye drops. I always made several copies for her ER doctors just in case they didn't have the growing list. TIP: Copies should be kept in the home, car, and in your pocket if you have a patient visiting the ER once or twice a week. I made it a habit to make copies at the local library once the prescriptions reached three drugs or more. If you can't remember the names of the drugs, it is time to make a few copies for the doctors and nurses.

I immediately called her sister to report her trip to the hospital. As the ambulance was about to leave, a medic walked towards me and asked, "Did you know she's incoherent?" I said in sarcastic manner, "Yeah, she was released from a psychiatric hospital seven days ago. She is using your ambulance as a way to wander and it really upsets our family!" Mom is scared of her psychiatrist for some reason and thinks she is going to see him next Monday. She is going to see her primary-care doctor on Monday. I briefly described what had happened so the driver could type her history into his laptop: "Her psychiatrist kicked her out of his office last Thursday. She is still mad and that is why she wants to go to the

ER. My mother politely told the psychiatrist she couldn't do any of the things he requested. "Ms. Dollie, I see no reason why you can't sit in the Sun for a few minutes each day," He said. She replied, "No doctor, I can't walk!" He goes on, "I can't see any problem that would prevent you from walking in your yard." I want you out of the "Big Chair" and in the yard as often as possible. He asked, "Ms.Dollie, can you do that for me?" She didn't reply!

I mentioned to the driver, "Our family has been trying to get her out of that chair for years and it sounds too good to be true!" But once again, she repeated, "No, I can't walk!" I saw a grimace on the doctor's face followed by some deep breathing. Soon, I knew what was "coming down the pike and it wasn't going to be good!" But, that's mom, I thought to myself. I could tell her doctor had heard enough! He knew my mother didn't have the slightest inclination to get well! She would be an outcast in her group of friends—the first one to get well and feel great! No one felt great in mom's group of friends and she couldn't have good news for her friends.

Mom's Wednesday night ER records got to the psychiatrist before her appointment last Thursday. The ER doctors, a week earlier, had diagnosed nausea and it upset her psychiatrist.

He said, "I have a lot of respect for doctors, but Ms. Dollie, "No one ever died of nausea that I can recall!" This statement concerning nausea upset mom so much that she stopped using "abdominal pain" as her primary ruse to wander-by- ambulance; she used "stroke" in her last trip to the ER.

My sister and I thought someone was prompting mother before each trip to the ER. I called a dozen "phone-buddies" and never could get any proof. Mom asked a strange question: Did you hire that psychiatrist to make me mad? I replied, "No, I hired him to help you get well!" People can die from Alzheimer's and I want you to stay well so you can take care of Sarah and Daisy for a long time. That was the first time I ever mentioned Alzheimer's was a fatal disease to mother.

I told the ambulance driver, who was now next to a medic listening to my story about mom's last trip to her psychiatrist, I want her taken to the Behavioral Hospital. Can you take her where she wandered Monday night with you guys?" The Behavioral Hospital has her records and I want to talk to the Intake Counselor about abusing ambulances, doctors, and ER's. They may want her admitted tonight or early in the morning. He didn't reply, but shook his head in the affirmative and looked away. I thought since I mentioned a prominent hospital in the area, the driver wouldn't dare take her elsewhere! After making a few calls and checking the house, I drove to the Behavioral Hospital. The snow had melted and the roads were clearing. I waited in the Behavioral Hospital's Night Clinic for more than an hour before leaving. I drove straight home because the roads were clear.

I called all hospitals in the area and the three new ones within five miles. The all replied, "No, we do not have her!" Finally, we called the ambulance company and they told us they dropped her off at the Heart Hospital three hours ago! Why is the Heart Hospital lying to me?

I called the Heart Hospital for a second time only to hear she hasn't been admitted for a second time." I asked, "The ambulance company just told me they dropped her off at 5 p.m. They repeated for a third time, "Well, she isn't on my sheet!" I gathered my thoughts and figured that everybody is lying at the Heart Hospital, but wasn't sure why!

I drove to the Heart Hospital's ER and they repeated, "She isn't here two more times!" I thought somebody was running me in circles and something was really wrong, but for some reason I couldn't get a handle on the ordeal. I started to feel like a second-class citizen with no rights or privileges to see my mother. The ER had no information for me and it was an eerie feeling for a caregiver to experience.

All of a sudden, I recognized a neighbor walking in the parking lot. As I walked to my car, I ran into Judy, our neighbor two houses down the road. I said, "Have you seen my mother?" She said, your mother just called from this hospital and asked, "Come visit me!" I told Judy, "I thought someone was lying to me for some reason." Judy replied, "Follow me to the emergency room, but wait outside and I'll see what is going on." As Judy walked towards the emergency room, she started laughing as she told me what mom told the ER staff after mom arrived:

Don't call her four kids because they live in California and they would be mad if they knew she was in the hospital. Actually, Mom has only three kids and her two daughters live in Houston and Waco.

I got the feeling that Judy had been to the ER before I met her in the parking lot. When Judy said, "Wait here and I'll see what is going on in the ER was my cue that she was helping mom "escape!" I didn't have mom's contract from the Behavioral Hospital with me to show to the ER staff. When mom became agitated, she was required to go to any emergency room and direct them to take her to the Behavioral Hospital as soon as possible.

I waited for almost an hour in the hallway and Judy never came back. I left because it was getting close to 11 p.m. I knew our neighbor had something to do with mom missing. Why would Judy endanger mom's health and well being by not reporting her recent hospitalization to the ER?

I believe the Deputy had already taken mom to ADULT CARE, INC. and Judy had already left the hospital without telling me! I couldn't imagine Judy helping my mother without asking our family or the nurses at the Behavioral Hospital. Judy had told the Deputy that mom was afraid to live with me! I believe the officer left with mom before I got to the ER that night. After I refused to give the officer her four medications at 8 p.m., the officer drove mom to ADULT CARE, INC. He had no intentions of telling me his reason for showing up at 8 p.m. that night. I wasn't allowed to read his report for that evening because I was the accused in the case. I believe Judy had visited the ER several times that night—she lives just three miles away. Mom started her "danger" drama and Judy agreed she was in danger because she believed mom's "delusional stories."

Unfortunately, the public doesn't know anything about Alzheimer's. In the first three stages of the disease, patients seem quite normal and even doctors have difficulty diagnosing the disease. It is rare for Alzheimer's patients to be placed into a nursing home before Stage-5. Since mom was in Stage-3 at the time of her last wandering, it was too early to see her off to a nursing facility. It was about twenty-miles to ADULT

CARE, INC. Furthermore, that was the approximate distance to mom's Behavioral Hospital where she should have been admitted that night.

I was in that hospital waiting for the ambulance to arrive. She would be shuttled to her old room if the ambulance had taken my request seriously. If she were admitted, there would have been no PO, no nursing home, and she would have gotten the care she needed in four to eight weeks. Finally, this book wouldn't have been written and well over sixty complaints wouldn't have been filed in this case. However, this state would still have a serious problem with caregivers. Judy is a good example of strangers doing Alzheimer's and doing it badly! Judy is an example of people who do not know about the early stages of Alzheimer's—they are familiar with only the late-stages (stages 6 and 7) of the disease!

What bothered me was the fact that Judy was present and laughed when mother told the ER about her four kids. Evidently, Judy didn't know my mother was in the "suspicion-phase" of Alzheimer's and believed mother's horrible stories. Judy didn't realize or cared about mom being delusional while in this dangerous phase of Alzheimer's. TIP: In reality, people not close to the patient can't understand why someone mentioned California in the same sentence with having four kids. Both statements are delusional!

Likewise, the words "being in danger" had a no valid meaning to Judy and the Heart Hospital that night. Paranoia is a type of delusion in which a person believes that others are lying and "out to get them."

Mom told the ER staff her son made her see a psychiatrist that she hated, made her take her pills, and locked the doors so she couldn't wander the neighborhood at night. These previous statements were the crux of mom's complaint to ask for a PO. Mom was mad at her doctor and me! She started her drama at the Heart Hospital—I am in danger! I am in danger!

Curiously, these so-called Alzheimer's professionals, took the bait, hook, line, and sinker—this uneducated behavior classifies them as: Strangers doing Alzheimer's. This state has to pass laws to restrict such behavior from strangers trying to so-call "help" Alzheimer's patients.

The Heart Hospital said they had absolutely no recourse but to call the Sheriff. This officer came to my house at 8 p.m. and wanted her medicine because he had already made up his mind to take mother to ADULT CARE, INC. He had no intentions to take mother to the hospital she was released eight days ago! My first e-mail to this officer mentioned the name of the hospital so he couldn't confuse where she was released. Mother spent the night in an ADULT CARE, INC. safe house! One big problem: ADULT CARE, INC. safe house had no heater.

After spending several days under supervision of ADULT CARE, INC., they asked mom to write a check for her lodging. Yes, it made mom mad, but she couldn't do anything about the accommodations— she was responsible for her behavior. Mom couldn't write a check so someone did it for her and she signed her name. And, I was in the same town renting motel and hotel rooms for the ten days preceding the court hearing. My bills totaled almost $1,200 for the ten days.

I wasn't allowed to live in our house for those two weeks, even though mom spent much of her time in a safe house and in at least two nursing homes. My Internet businesses dropped off the face of the Earth for those ten days. What kind of state prevents caregivers from making a living while helping a loved one?

Our two dogs, Sarah and Daisy, suffered because no one gave them food or water for five days. I wanted to file on the judge and ADULT CARE, INC. that kept food and water from our pets. I called ADULT SERVICES and complained to "DD" about the animal situation. She got a Alice to feed and water them on the sixth day. We think ADULT SERVICES and ADULT CARE, INC. should have been prosecuted for animal cruelty.

I hadn't been to court, and didn't know where to find the judge. Also, the court refused to give me the police report. The first judge that signed the PO wrote his name in a way that even my attorney didn't know who he was. The judge wrote his complete name in the same rolling letters— it looked like a row of small hills—what a professional?

A month later, I glanced at the Heart Hospital's paperwork after filing a formal complaint against them. The form showed mom had no health problems the night she wandered to their ER. This was the case for all previous excursions. If mom took an ambulance to the hospital and got no treatment for "stroke," can't someone infer maybe something is wrong here!

Perhaps the patient is mentally ill and needs to be evaluated by a mental-health professional. This is the best a modern hospital can do—place her in a safe house and quickly institutionalize her for being in Stage-3 Alzheimer's. That is the most absurd thing I have ever heard in my life. The family had no say in the matter—Stage-3 is nothing to worry about if you have an experienced caregiver running the "show" and proper locks are installed.

At office visits, I could see her psychiatrist trying his best to discourage mother to "STOP WANDERING!" He yelled at her twice, but it never soaked into mom's brain. He looked mom in the face and said, "It is too dangerous for someone your age!" However, she never got the message and I hate to say, that's how mom lived her life. She left the doctor's office sobbing and vowing never to come back to his clinic.

Before the Thursday-night trip, I begged the "Monday-night doctors to keep her overnight, but they couldn't because she had no serious health problem. Finally, I asked if I could take her home? Mom looked around as if she were alarmed at my question. Mom questioned if they should release her at all since she arrived very sick. Her attitude didn't persuade the doctors and nurses and they quickly replied, "Give her stomach a few minutes to adjust to the medication, then we will release her so she can go home." She didn't want to go home because she was receiving too much attention in the ER.

She craved all the attention in the hospital ER Monday night. The doctor's were making wandering fun and exciting. She enjoyed the attention and there would be many conversations with her friends next week—how the hospital staff worked feverishly to stop the spread of nausea. It was hard for me to keep from laughing-out-loud.

She looked at me asking the same question over and over, "You are not going to hurt me, are you?" She repeated it over and over and the doctors and nurses stared. The staring had to be answered: "No one is going to hurt you! I looked toward the doctors and assured them, "She just got out of your Behavior Hospital five days ago for dementia. I asked, "Is it possible to move her tonight?" Mom could get the rest she needs there? Mom quickly responded to that question: "Oh, No! I want to go home and sleep in my bed with my dogs."

Fortunately, I started carrying the letter from her psychiatrist in my pocket. It was folded in my wallet and I handed it to the physician in charge. The following is a modified version of the letter to me:

During this admission, she has not demonstrated appropriate insight into her illness or shown intact judgment regarding decisions involving her own care.

Given her level of functioning at this time, I would recommend that an appropriate guardianship be put into place for her protection and care.

Doctor's signature and date.

This was the first time my mother ever used the words "hurt me" and I started to wonder who "prompted" her with such language. She has never been abused and I was cautious after that statement. Neighbors and friends thought she should go back to the hospital for at least four weeks. I nixed the idea until I could talk to the insurance company. They hadn't paid her bill, even though her doctor okayed the visit. I worried about the growing debt and mom going back for many weeks.

CH. 16 PROTECTIVE ORDER ARRIVES

At 10:30 p.m., two Sheriff Deputies presented a Protective Order. I was startled that I had to get some things and leave at such a late hour. One officer had looked for mom on several occasions. He said he lived in the neighborhood and I could call or e-mail him if I needed help. He handed me his business card that had two e-mail addresses. On two occasions, he searched our neighbor's house and finally located her. But, tonight he and his partner were more serious than I thought they should be. Abuse seemed to be at the top of their list. No laughing and joking tonight; they were terse with me. We had an odd feeling about this officer showing up so many times in his Sheriff's car. I never called him, but neighbors called to report mom's wandering behavior to their homes. She scared neighbors by mentioning a Mexican living with us! I never wanted the officer to help find mother—he had a personality that bothered me.

We were upset with him since he wanted to question mom in a closet at a neighbor's house without my presence. I sent the officer two e-mails questioning his motivation and emotional attachment to the case. I never trusted him to make a good decision with my mother. Finally, I wrote him a second email questioning his integrity and hoped that would end our short friendship! We all hunted mom in and around a ¼-mile circle. The officer didn't know mom's car keys were in our safe and her dementia prevented her from opening that safe. The trust wasn't there and I wanted to tell him we didn't need his help anymore. As mom's caregiver, my intuition turned out to be accurate about this officer—he had no common sense! The Heart Hospital had called this Deputy and he called ADULT CARE, INC. with full knowledge of mom's recent hospitalization from my first e-mail. The officer's reaction was a poor decision for mom and our family! I immediately got an appointment to see his boss and explain mom's health and behavior. I told his boss the officer refused to do the right thing and wanted, for some reason, to escalate the situation.

Our mother needed further treatment at the Behavioral Hospital. She never got the treatment she needed because this officer made a bad choice that night to escalate the situation. My question is "Why escalate?" How can mom help write a PO when she was delusional and hallucinating on that last trip to the ER? The family wondered, "Why didn't she go to the Behavioral Hospital instead of them searching for an assisted-living home for weeks?"

I gathered clothes, shoes, computer, medication, razor, and toothbrush. I told the officers something wasn't right with this P.O. My mother couldn't have written these statements because the medic on the ambulance told me mother was incoherent when they left Thursday afternoon.

Finally, I looked towards both officers and said, "Oh yes, here it is, these sentences show she is delusional. Her writing skills had deteriorated over the past six months and I typed all of her communications. Further, at the psychiatric hospital, she couldn't write a sentence longer than four words.

The Officers seem to be impatient at my ability to gather things and leave. I was asleep when they arrived. One officer said "Someone could have written the PO for her." I replied, "Well that makes sense!" I quickly added, "I see the initials DD next to the fabricated statements. Who is DD and where does she work?" They looked at my mother's statement on the P.O. and guessed, "It is probably the person who wrote it for your mother." These officers knew who wrote the PO for mom because the same ADULT CARE, INC. is used by all the deputies in that county. I became suspicious of their lies and was careful what I said around them. He never cared for my mother or her family.

The following is an exact copy of what my mother reported to the social worker the next day at ADULT CARE, INC. It is called the "description of incidents" which caused the filing of the petition for protection.

Additionally, instructions were given to the person writing the description: Describe what happened, when and where the event(s) occurred. List all actions or behaviors you intend to present to the court at the hearing:

About 1 wk ago, J.P. was mad he said I can't believe you, You are just a no good son of a b---h of a mother no one would miss you if you died tonight. J.P. keeps the doors locked so I can't even get out to sit in the Sun like my doctor said to. I can tell he can't stand me. He is supposed to take care of me and won't. Yesterday I thought I was having a stroke because of the stress of living with him. I pushed my emergency button and told them I was in danger get here fast the ambulance came & took me to the hospital.

Written by "DD" Advocate, permission of Ms. Dollie.

As I gathered my personal things to leave the home, one officer asked, "As you go through your stuff, you are not going to accidentally find a handgun are you?" I thought it might be a good time to mention I fished with their Chief of Police. But, I decided not to and hoped nothing would cause an unfortunate accident.

I was scared of the officer I had e-mailed twice because his latest performance proved to me he definitely had some sort of problem understanding Alzheimer's behaviors.

Mom lost the ability to write a check about a year ago when she saw people roaming her kitchen. She was losing her car keys twice a day. Finally, I asked her to leave the keys on the table so we wouldn't lose them. She thought all the people walking through the house would steal the keys and then her car. She said, "Someone is going to steal my Ford Taurus from the garage if I don't find a safe place for my car keys! I called the insurance company to ask if they had full coverage on the car and they said, "Yes!"

Mom had a serious problem with her car next to my business. She reminded me that the man down the road offered her lots of money for her Ford because it had only 30,000 miles on it. The car was fifteen-years old and sitting created many mechanical problems. I hid her keys so that she couldn't wander in it. We used the excuse that I was the one who lost her car keys. She told friends that J.P. lost the keys and we ride in his Toyota to the lake to feed the ducks. She ask me to contact the locksmith and I repeated that it would cost $100 to make a key. You don't need any keys, I'll take you where you need to go. Finally, I made one key without her knowledge and kept it in my pocket. I didn't want her to wander in her car and that was a growing threat if she could get her hands on a key. I never told the Deputy that mom had no access to car keys.

Mom began questioning me about all the people walking through the house. My Internet business was next to the garage. I reminded her that neighbors and friends weren't allowed to just walk through. My product is manufactured by highly-sensitive presses—a slight movement of any kind could damage the final product. Visitors were routed through the front door and never through the garage while the press was working! Her questioning caused alarm and we called her doctor for an appointment. I reassured her that the doors were locked and strangers weren't walking through the house. Even though my business was in her garage, products were made in the homes of the workers I hired. They all got a press installed in their home to cut the papers. Each worker was responsible for shipping orders to the customer. I took orders, made invoices, ordered supplies, and e-mailed employees. I had a press near my desk and occasionally cut a few papers just for fun. Strangers didn't come and go as mom suggested. She continued to hallucinate about people in the kitchen up to that final Thursday.

The door locks in our home had to have keys on the inside to lock them. This format was mandatory before the Behavioral Hospital allowed mom to come home. We left the keys in the lock and turned the key to open the doors. However, if the key was used to lock the door and then removed, mom would have to have a key to open the door. Social Workers asked me to contact them when everything was completed.

This locking system was easy to set up and mom couldn't walk away at night without a key. The sliding door at the back of the house had a block of wood in the runners to prevent mom from opening the sliding-glass door. The back door was problematic since it had a flip-lock on the door. This was mom's favorite exit and the hospital wanted it changed.

The hospital wanted me to change this lock to an key-locking system similar to the one on our front door. Also, they wanted the garage-door button removed and use only the remotes to open and close the garage door. The remotes would be stored on the dresser in my room at the end of each day, so that mom couldn't access them without my knowledge.

CH. 17 YELLING BEHAVIOR AND STAGES

Friends and relatives couldn't believe mom wandered five times because we all thought that Alzheimer's progressed at a slow pace. We all thought it would be years before mom would be wandering, if at all. She wandered three times on foot to homes within 100 yards of our house. Neighbors were calling the police before I could tell them she had Stage-3 Alzheimer's.

I remember the Deputy asking, "What was going on just minutes before she walked away tonight?" I said, "Officer, I recall she needed to see her psychiatrist about using ambulances to wander to ER's. Officer, she never got along with her psychiatrist and I worry she may need his care.

Suddenly, I wondered, "Why would a police officer play detective when he should know Alzheimer's patients aren't normal? The questions this officer asked proved he had no knowledge of the disease. Also, his questions put me on edge and my trust in him soon disappeared! How would an officer solve a case when Alzheimer's behavior is considered "nonsense" by the medical establishment! If he were properly trained, he should know about dementia and Alzheimer's erratic behavior! Who trains these officers?

The alarm would always go off when mom wandered-by-foot. When I heard the alarm, I knew it wasn't an intruder; mom forgot the code and was wandering again! The dogs started barking and they wanted outside to see what mom was doing. The alarm code was mom's birthday (2-24-30), but her memory was questionable at night and didn't bother turning it off when she left. She refused to allow the dogs to follow. I never asked her why she didn't let the dogs run with her, but danger was likely the reason. Mom didn't realize the danger she was exposing herself walking the streets in the dark.

About a month before mom's last wandering, a friend of mine called our home phone and asked for me. Mom didn't recognize his voice and immediately "yelled" at him over the phone. She repeated, "Help, I need help, I need help!" This yelling was a shock to me because it was her first time to yell at a friend of mine. I explained her diagnosis to the caller and he reassured me this was a similar experience with his family. Mom started yelling at people on the phone. A caregiver told me it was common for Alzheimer's patients to yell at people in Stage 3 Alzheimer's. She reminded me that some patients develop forms of agitation and restlessness that include yelling behavior. Could she be experiencing verbal aggression along with delusions at the same time?

Every week brought new and unusual behavior and questions. She would never yell at anybody on the phone a few months ago. Caregivers must remember it is easy to misinterpret what you see and hear.

TIP: "All behavior is communication" is a statement that is repeated dozens of times at seminars and meetings, but it must be carefully evaluated. Remember,

Alzheimer's patients are in different stages of the disease. The doctor gave her a prescription for anxiety and depression to see if it would work for her. When I could get her to take the medicine, her behavior was great—she enjoyed food, her dogs, and talking to friends.

Changes in communication and the ability to communicate can vary and are based on the person and where he or she is "in" the disease:

In Early stage of Alzheimer's, an individual is still able to participate in give-and-take dialogue, have meaningful conversations and engage in social activities. In Early stage of Alzheimer's he or she may repeat stories, have difficulty finding the right word or feel overwhelmed by excessive stimulation. TIP: Talk slowly and look directly at your loved one.

In Middle Stage of Alzheimer's, is typically the longest and can last for many years. As the disease progresses, the person will have greater difficulty communicating and will require more direct care.

In <u>Late Stage of Alzheimer's</u> disease may last from several weeks to several years. As the disease advances, the person with Alzheimer's may rely on nonverbal communication such as facial expressions or vocal sounds. Around-the-clock care is usually required in this stage.

TIPS FOR SUCCESSFUL COMMUNICATION

- Treat the person with dignity and respect. Avoid talking down to the person or talking as if he or she isn't there.
- Approach the person from the front and identify yourself.
- Encourage nonverbal communication. If you don't understand what is being said, ask the person to point or gesture.
- Sometimes the emotions being expressed are more important than what is behind the words or sounds.
- Use touch, sights, sounds, smells and tastes as a form of communication with the person.

It is OK if you don't know what to do or say; your presence and friendship are most important.

CH. 18 CAREGIVER IN ANOTHER STATE

I was working and living in southern Missouri four years ago. Mom called and said she was sick. Of the three kids, I was closest to mom's home. I was teaching chemistry in a high school and running my business in my spare time. It was near the end of the school day and the principal reported my mother sounded desperate. The next morning, I drove to her home and checked her appearance and food supply. I found an enormous stock of cakes, cookies, brownies, pies, corn chips, and ice cream. She had a lunch contract with Meals on Wheelsâ and I knew she always had a good lunch. Her complaints seem to center on being tired of the these meals. Mom could still drive to the store and buy her groceries and dog food. It didn't take long to determine she had the frig full of snacks and all this junk food irritated her stomach and gave her acid reflux.

I called a friend that talked to my mother on a daily basis. Annie told me mother had stopped cooking for herself over six months ago. Mom told Annie she snacked and didn't feel like cooking for one person. However, she was capable of going grocery shopping and cooking small meals. But, it was starting to become a challenge for her and I didn't know what was going on with her health. I decided to buy the groceries and prepare both lunch and dinner. We dropped Meals on Wheels a month later. She was happy to hear the good news. I ask her to continue with Meals on Wheels until I could make a decision about her health and mental condition. I made a doctor's appointment later that day for a check up.

I called the school in Missouri and resigned. Later, I moved into a room in her house. Mother was still capable of writing checks and paying her bills on her own. Also, mom was capable of driving her dogs to the Vet and having them groomed and cared for without my help. My concerns centered around early-stage Alzheimer's; however, it would be another three years before we had a definitive answer.

Mom's memory was fair and our family didn't question her relatives or neighbors about any health problems. I wanted to make sure her health was good before making any plans. She had gained almost 20 lbs. since January, almost nine months ago. I thought exercise would be part of her agenda for getting her health back to normal.

The sugary diet and no exercise was some concern for her new doctor. A nurse collected blood and urine samples. These tests can identify disorders such a anemia, infection, diabetes, kidney, liver disease, vitamin deficiencies, thyroid problems, and problems with heart and lungs. He quickly discovered a urinary track infection (UTI). But, the doctor had good news: Everything was normal range for her age except the infection.

However, the doctor mentioned a UTI can cause confused thinking, trouble focusing attention, memory problems or other symptoms. Alzheimer's (AHLZ-high-merz) disease immediately popped into my mind because of her age and her father dying from the disease. Her mother had the disease, but died of uterine cancer.

According to the Alzheimer's Association, there are almost a dozen forms of dementia. Dementia is a general term for the loss of memory and other intellectual abilities serious enough to interfere with daily life. Alzheimer's, which is the most common form of dementia accounting for 60 to 80 percent of the cases. That includes 11 percent of those age 65 and older and one- third of those 85 and older.[13]

CH. 19 HEALTH FROM FUSE BOXES

Mom had fair health throughout life. She had her thyroid removed at age thirty because of cancer. When my parents divorced, grandpa owned a telephone business and did part-time electrical work in the community. In his late 50's he would take me with him and I worked hard to be a good companion and helper. I was about ten-years-old and had a great memory—something he needed. On one occasion, grandpa overheard me telling grandma that I had memorized large passages of the Bible. After a short display of my work, grandpa made me his right-hand man. He never left the house without me. He stopped using notebooks and journals and made me responsible for keeping track of the electrical inventory and orders.

Grandpa had problems with his memory in his fifties and occasionally became upset. He would suddenly stop the truck and with a red face, "Damn it, I forgot my list again! We would spend part of the day driving back and forth in his Dodge Pickup. He used pencil and paper for his memory loss, but later used my memory to recall minute details of work orders. Grandpa had problems ordering parts and wiring for homes. His math and memory skills were becoming serious problems and he knew it! This man was admitted to Washington D.C. Law School and New York Medical School but his dementia crippled his ability to calculate receipts for his customers.

For some reason, grandpa began questioning clients about their infidelity. Memory loss and confusion may cause a person with Alzheimer's to perceive things in new and unusual ways. Individuals may become suspicious of those around them, even accusing others of theft, infidelity or other improper behavior. Sometimes a person may misinterpret what he or she sees and hears.[14]

All of a sudden grandpa sounded like a "preacher with a poor memory!" At ten years old, I didn't know or cared what "shacking up" meant, but it was bantered often. He hated a Mr. Osborn because he was "shacking up" with Pam. Pam was Grandpa's favorite customer because she always paid in cash! He often commented about Pam's misshapen nose and how beautiful she would be with a normal shape. Grandpa told me Mr. Osborn was married when he was with Pam. It took years to put the puzzle pieces together on my mother's side of the family. Looking back at some of the things grandpa said and did in his late fifties, it was easy to see Alzheimer's wasn't the only secret he battled most of his life.

> We headed for town once a month to buy supplies. It was lots of fun for me help with his ordering. I believe Grandpa's colleagues noticed he had some form of dementia. No one knew anything about memory problems in the fifties. His best friends and colleagues called him unique and novel.

> I believe these terms were used because of his battle with memory loss. I remember everyone calling him "shorty." He was about five-feet three-inches tall and heavyset. Grandpa needed me to keep track of all the different sizes of wire used for homes and businesses—I had no trouble ordering enough to last a month. I was excited to go to town because he would take mineral baths at a hotel. After the bath and massage, I started complaining that I wanted a hamburger, some fries, and a Pepsi. He said, "No to all three!"

Grandpa was a ferocious businessman—he owned three grocery stores near Salina. He owned a motel early in his career. Later, he owned a telephone company at Twin Oaks. Finally, he was a part-time farmer and electrician. I was fortunate he had time to baby sit and do his electrical work. My memory never failed him. He would ask me to recall what a certain client wanted done in their homes. I would quickly reply, "Grandpa, he wanted a fuse box in his garage."

On one particular day during the summer, I remember grandpa driving back to our house in an angry mood. His dementia was taking its toll on his memory and personality. I remember this gentle man saying, "If I could catch who is stealing my fuse boxes, I would shoot them!" I was too scared to say anything! I wanted to ask who would want to steal rusty boxes stacked inside our garage?" Also, we piled up electrical supplies inside the garage and it was difficult for me to dig them from the pile. I wondered who would be brave enough to walk into our garage and steal fuse boxes! Grandpa gave me a second job: "Keep an eye open for thieves!"

Grandpa did carry a gun but kept its location a secret because he was afraid I would find it. I looked many times when he was gone, but he had the gun well hidden. I didn't know at the time it was the disease talking and kids didn't care about diseases.

My grandpa lived with the disease until he died at ninety-seven. I was in my forties when he passed from the disease. He lived a long and healthy life; He never consumed alcohol, drugs, or tobacco. His electrical work was strenuous and these factors could have helped him cope with the Alzheimer's disease for a long time.

> My mother mentioned she noticed fits-of-anger when she was working in his stores. Her memory centered around being poor and having little to eat in the Depression Days. Nothing could be further from the truth. Her mother and dad bartered for fresh game from a constant supply of people needing canned foods from grandpa's three stores.

CH. 20 STRANGERS AND THE PROTECTIVE ORDER

In late Spring, I received a certified letter from a law firm. The following was my response to a list of actions they demanded:

RE: Ms. Dollie vs. J.P. Ripple; County Court

Dear Mr. Ripple:

I represent Ms. Dollie regarding the above mentioned case. I also represent Ms. Dollie in all other matters relating to her residence, her vehicle, her dogs and her personal property. Be advised that this letter is notice to you to vacate the residence located (Left out) on or before midnight (date left out).

This Residence is owned by my client Ms. Dollie through her trust.

Sincerely, Law Firm.

I e-mailed my response:

Dear Sir:

I would like to remind you that Judge declared the utilities not be disconnected during the time I am in the house. The Judge knows I run an Internet business from our garage and I will contact him immediately if these utilities are stopped. I plan to vacate the residence in three months, as the court directed. If you will read the PO, the dogs belong to me. My mother gave them to me in court and the final PO verifies this statement.

However, I will give the dogs back if the utilities are not interrupted during my stay. The only time I drove my Mom's car was to have it serviced at Bill's Tire Co. The fifteen-year-old car wouldn't run. Therefore, I asked them to repair it and they cleaned the injectors and fuel system.

The bill was $100. If Ms. Dollie would like to refund this money, I will get a receipt for the work. Finally, the letter I sent my mother was a letter that had to be opened and attended to immediately! I didn't know her SSN, health account number, or health insurance ID number.

There were no minutes recorded in court for this PO, so you will have to believe my notes. I wanted to see who was instigating this action by an attorney. Finally, I am her son and she hallucinates about a fat man and a Mexican living with us. I am the best person to take care of her because I was trained in the Army and worked closely with the Army Health Nurse to follow-up on cases of abuse and secure proper nutrition for children living on military bases.

Sincerely, J.P. Ripple.

CH. 21 MY FAMILY HISTORY

Mom's dad and uncle left Monterey, TN in 1917. Her dad and uncle were both in their late twenties. Mom's dad, Dave Blaylock, suggested they drive west to escape the law. Dave had an affair with a woman in Monterey and her husband came home unannounced. Dave ran from the house and pulled his pistol and shot at the man as he grabbed Dave's shirt. The shot missed and hit a washtub hanging on a nail at the side of the house. The muffled sound convinced Dave he shot the husband. Early next day, the wife's cousin located Dave and Jim at their mother's house. He had planned a scheme to get Dave out of Tennessee for good. He told Dave that he had killed Busby and the law was looking for him. The bogus story caused Dave and Jim to leave Tennessee permanently. Dave was working part-time for a telephone company to pay for medical school. Neither notified relatives about leaving nor their plans. Thirty years later, Mary Blaylock told friends her sons left that day and never contacted her again. In her memoirs, Mary said, "I waited on the porch, in my rocking chair, fifteen years for Dave to come home!"

Dave and Jim spent only a short time in their hometown of Monterey. They had attended Washington D.C. Law School, but a fire destroyed the building and their apartment. A year later, Dave returned to Monterey to work the summer to pay for his first year at N.Y. Medical School. The affair forced Dave to leave town and forget a medical career.

> Dave and Jim drove west until they were exhausted. They stopped and spent time in Harrison, Arkansas. At that point, they decided to separate. Dave was the primary suspect, so he decided to take a train to Indian Territory; however, Jim decided to take a train to Chicago. The only thing left was to say goodbye and promise to contact each other when things cool off. Jim told Ms. Dollie at a rare meeting in 1957, "He and Dave rarely communicated during those years!"

Dave headed for Chouteau, Oklahoma by train. He took a different train to Kenwood, Oklahoma the next day. Years later, Dave married Stella Crawford in Kenwood. They built a house north of town. He changed his name to Dave Young because of his brother and the law. However, mail was constantly confused with his neighbor with the same surname. Therefore, Dave Young split his last name to just part of Young: "oung part."

He had no choice but to keep the "Y" so his brother could contact him. In 1924, Dave Y. Oung lived next door to the Young's and got his mail on time. Dave's brother, Jim Young, waited in Chicago for Dave to report any change in his brother's dilemma.

Dave liked Chouteau so much that he bought the only motel in 1940. It is still standing with a weathered-Monterey marquee. He bought an acre of land on the east side of town with money left over from the motel deal.

He told relatives that the one-acre of land was used for investment purposes. However, Dave rented it to his business partner on a 99-year lease.

He and Stella had a son who died during birth in 1926. My mother was born, Dollie J. Oung in 1930. Mom's only sister Priscilla L. Oung was born in 1936.

Dave Y. Oung decided to tell his family about his misadventures when mom was twenty-five. Priscilla said it caused anxiety in the immediate family. They tolerated the news, but she said it was problematic throughout their lives. The secret was kept until his death at 97. He was notified by his estranged-Tennessee family that his shot missed Jim Busby. I remember Grandpa saying in a relieved manner, "I always thought I killed him!"

CH. 22 MOM'S HEALTH IN THE 1970'S

On September 30, 1970, I was drafted into the Army via a lottery system. My number was 205. The Vietnam War was still raging at the time.

In the spring of 1970, I dropped out of college for a semester to job hunt. I had changed my major from biology to chemistry and felt confident the "Army Lotto" wouldn't reach my number. My goal was to be a top chemist for either the government or the oil business. The government was hiring so I took a part-time job without thinking about the ongoing war. The job transferred me to a small lake. My new job was to analyze water in the swimming areas of the lake. The job wasn't exactly what I had planned with my chemistry degree, but the pay and benefits were excellent.

> However, on July 20th the lottery was creeping up on my number and I called the draft board in panic. The news was bad! The reply: "Yes, we are thinking it will go to 210 in the few months, but definitely 210 by the end of the year. I wasn't enrolled in college and that was a sweet deferment for the last four years. I remember telling my boss it might be a "Harry" Christmas for me!

I eventually volunteered on September 1, 1970 with two of my friends. The pressure was too much working a full-time job at the lake. My mother was very upset and I worried about her mental health for months.

Once the three of us signed up and left home, we never saw each other again. Both of my friends were disabled during the War. I made a high score my IQ test and the Army transferred me to San Antonio, Texas to the Brook Army Hospital. Ft. Sam Houston had the best "Water Lab" school in the Service. I was close to a second degree in chemistry by a few hours and was being trained at one of the largest labs in the country.

My plans included finishing the degree in the service and working on an idea that later turned into my first patent in chemistry. I planned to leave the service with four college degrees. Also, the nurses were numerous and I thought marrying a nurse would be a good thing for me. The family housing at Ft. Sam Houston was much better than the Army barracks.

During this time, my mother questioned the Army taking her only son. I was studying for my MOS (military occupation skill) at Ft. Sam Houston, and didn't know she was having so many emotional problems. My step-dad would drive from their home to San Antonio to spent a day visiting at he barracks. I wrote mom often to remind her my job wasn't that dangerous—"I am working in a laboratory most of the time," I told her. Dad called once in a while to report he thought she was having hallucinations and mini-strokes, especially at night!

In those days, you could drive your car to the barracks and just walk in. Mom's letters were always full of anxiety and agitation. She cried often during calls. However, everyone got letters full of anxiety and sadness during the war. But, mom's health seem to be going downhill fast!

Finally, I talked to my commanding officer about her mini-strokes and being the only son. He was against the war and asked me to visit a captain who was a chaplain. He wanted me to go the CO (conscientious objector) route. I decided against this approach because it would take about a year to complete. A ten-page essay would have to be submitted and I just didn't feel like writing my way out of the war.

He was straight forward with me— it would be easy for me to get released from service. I was the only son and he thought he could help. He reminded me that my MOS was in preventive medicine, and that group spent most of their time drinking Pepsi twenty miles behind the lines. I decided to listen to the commanding officer and stay in the service. I spent almost two years as a chemist at Ft. Riley, KS. President Nixon notified the generals that he was going to issue an order for some troops. The Army notified me I would qualify for one of President Nixon's executive orders.

Eventually, the order was changed to three-months and I stayed at Ft. Riley, KS until ETS. My company was released by the Army because they had an abundance of medics and water-field labs.

Mom had changed since my tour of duty. She smiled less and viewed the military as something to avoid at all costs. It took some time getting used to my "new" mom. Her face had a droopy appearance on its left side. It was noticeable in family pictures when I was still in the service. Mom had made it through another stressful period in her life, but stress was here to stay!

CH. 23 MOM'S HEALTH IN THE 1980'S

In 1985, my mother had a "Near Death Experience." She always wanted it published in book format, but never had the time. I always told her to publish it with her memoirs. She never had major surgery in her life. She did grieve for years about a growth on her inner ear might be cancer. Later, it turned out to be benign. The only cancer in mom's family was uterine, thyroid, and skin that her mother fought for years. Stella was a heavy user of tobacco "snuff" and the doctors in the 1950's warned her of the dangers of snorting Snuff.

Mom's thyroid surgery proved to be cancerous, but it was kept under control with medication. I always thought her thyroid was the major cause of her anxiety and depression in her life.

I watched the near death experience "stress" mom and the family for months. The following is a modified version of her near death experience:

"MY VISIT WITH JESUS"

> I had been shopping all day with a friend. I noticed a shortness of breath for about a week. Otherwise, that morning wasn't any different—I left the house early and picked up Kaye.

> We had breakfast and lunch at the same café. I had enough energy to shop until almost 3 p.m. I drove to my daughter's house about five miles away. I wanted to call my doctor, but decided not to when I arrived. My son got home from his classes soon after I got home. He took me to the nearest hospital that had a reputation for heart care. At 4 p.m., ER doctors thought it was a heart problem, but at age 55, they didn't seem that worried. They did call my primary-care doctor about

me being in the hospital ER. The ER doctors started an EKG and some nitroglycerin. All I can remember was an oxygen mask interfering with visiting with the doctors. The doctors were trying to communicate as they were moving me to the Cardiac Ward. They kept me for three days; my chest pain did stop. The nitro made me so sick to the stomach that I vomited several times the first night.

My sister came the second day to be with me. She knows I don't like being alone when I am very sick. She is a Christian and her deep faith and trust in God will pull me through. I didn't tell my sister about my experience for at least a week. I had a "death experience" in the ER that first day. My death experience was identical to a book I read a few weeks ago. The Pastor's account of his trip to Heaven was identical to mine.

I saw a mansion and the kingdom of God! Please friend, what I saw was real. Keep going to church and believe!

On the first day, they called in two heart specialists. They all huddled and decided to do a cardiac-catheterization procedure on me.

In about an hour, they came for me and I didn't know what to expect. I started praying to God: I want you to stand right here beside me. I am going to use my left hand as yours and I'll use my right hand as mine.They gave me a shot in the leg to numb it. Then, a small hole was made in my main artery. They slid something into my leg and into my heart. For some reason, I enjoyed seeing my heart on the monitor. I kept hearing the nurse tell the doctor I had a rash on my chest. I knew a rash was the first sign of being allergic to a medication. I started coughing and got dizzy. I could hear my blood pressure called out in the background. It is "dropping fast" was a warning carried throughout the room. It is 70/50 was the last thing I heard. I saw my body on the table and the nurses at my head. I went like a flash of light to Heaven. I was joyously excited, but blurted out, I'm dead! I thought of my family and how they would miss me. I had no worries, I was in a small cloud-like body that had no mass.

Never on Earth had I felt this total-emotional excitement—being with God. I felt like a child, peaceful, innocent, unburdened, unimpressed, curious, secure, and totally consumed with love. I took my time, I felt no sense of hurry, hurry, as I did on Earth. I can't remember hearing any music, but I do remember listening to something. I was so overwhelmed with love, joy, comfort, and peace. I looked at the floor and it was the whitest of white. The walls around me were white between' the floor and walls. The brightest lights came shining through. About ten inches up from the floor, the lights were gold colored. It felt so good at home with God. I didn't see anyone else in Heaven. It seemed that we had been communicating mind-to-mind.

God told me I'd be leaving now. I said, "I don't want to leave this peaceful place." He told me, "Yes, now, but for only a little while." He showed me a big, shining tunnel—there was light at my end only. There were about ten people with brown robes standing next to me. I looked at them to see if I knew any of them. I couldn't see any faces. They followed me into the tunnel. When I got to the end of the tunnel, I saw my spirit's cloud-like body come down into my body on the table below. The entire spirit was in the shape of a funnel directed into the top of my head.

Doctor's thought mom hallucinated from the drugs they used to deaden the pain in her leg. She came back to experience a horrible time in in the 1990's.

CH.24 FAMILY PROBLEMS IN THE 1990'S

Mom got involved in an adoption of an eighteen-month-old girl in 1995. Mom was 65 years old and still in good health. Family members thought she was delusional at the time and should stay out of the procedure. The child was placed for adoption by the child's mother. The mother had a history of drug abuse and already had two kids. The child's mother told Mom she wanted Jen adopted to a good family. My sister and her husband wanted to adopt another child. They had two sons and wanted two daughters to compliment their growing family. My sister asked my opinion on the adoption. I said, "I don't think she will be normal due to the drugs her mother took during pregnancy. My concerns were that the child would take funds from the others. In that case, I opposed the adoption.

> Eventually, they adopted Jen and a Korean baby. The two girls completed a family of six. Mom got involved in the child's adoption and it went through rather quickly. I ask Mom not to interfere in her daughter's adoption and let them do what needed to be done.

> A year later, the child seemed well adjusted to the growing family. The family was stretched for money and it was a difficult time for mom. I saw her give her best, but it wasn't good enough. She really needed medication for all the stress. At the time, mom's kids were attending college and spread out in Texas and Oklahoma. The problems with Jen persist after all those years for both families and some said the stress continued into the future! I saw mom taking medication for the stress and strain of adoption.

However, we warned mom not to meddle into her rearing. Grandparents can smother a growing family and their ideas may not suit the parents.

Nagging was prevalent during that time. Mom advised, "Your house is too small and you guys need more money in your savings!"

As Jen got older, she was placed in special education classes at school. She was diagnosed with some sort of defiant problems with teachers and family members. She carried these problems into he teen years—defiant problems can diminish a child's schooling and career. I called my sister to warn her about the problems that arise when mother's use drugs during pregnancy, but my message was too late. I never mentioned it again.

On one occasion, when Jen was 13-years-old, she accused the oldest brother of sexual misconduct. I recall the matter was bogus, but it strained the marriage and my mother's health. After years of court appearances, the lie was finally exposed by a special-education teacher and a school counselor. Jen's lies were exposed and their son got his life back!

Furthermore, the cost was tremendous for a family of six—well over $50,000 in legal fees. My mother grieved to this day over the adoption. I heard mom say on several occasions that she regretted the adoption and it was a big mistake in her life. Mom was hit again by a disturbance in her life that caused mental anguish for years.

Mom was heart broken after the state took Jen from the home and institutionalized the young girl. I believe Jen had a propensity to lie and used lying as a tool to solve problems. It is a common trait in abandoned teens and some use it very well. Several psychiatrists conferred she was a pathological liar and couldn't be trusted. Mom refused to look at the reports by experts and grieved in private. She never got over this adoption as far as I could see. Mom could never see both sides of a coin. Her unwilling attitude to work with her daughter resulted in a feud that remains today. Mom didn't get to see her grandkids because of her disagreeable behavior forced the family to move to a new home in Waco.

Eventually, Jen married and has three kids of her own. I believe mom suffered several mini-strokes during that period in her life. I am not a doctor, but I could see some sort of mental change in her life during that time. She seemed more depressed and confused than usual and we all felt sorry for her declining mental health.

Mom's health changed in the early nineties. She had a small growth on her inner ear. She had it removed using the laser-knife treatment. Mom's anxiety hit an all time high those years. The pea-sized tumor was discovered to be benign. The good news was a relief for everyone in the family, but the growth raised havoc for months. This benign tumor caused the worst anxiety I have ever seen in mom. Once the doctors mentioned a possible "balance" problem, mom immediately took advantage of the situation to stop walking. She told friends and relatives she couldn't walk anymore because she could fall. I think the fraudulent condition was a ruse so people would come and see her. It turned out to be a big mistake in her life. The "fake" condition isolated mom for years because her friends didn't want to visit someone who couldn't walk.

My step-dad finally succumb to cancer the following year. Mom and I were depressed for several days. Mom's possible heart problems and her inner ear nodule took backstage to dad's death. He battled leukemia for five years; he had been a smoker part of his life.

Mom took a turn for the worst when her youngest daughter's physical showed breast cancer in 2011. It was a roller-coaster ride for mom's mental health. Her daughter lived near M.D. Anderson and fought the cancer for two years and won. The family felt relieved as mom made it through another horrible round of "stress and strain."

CH 25 ALZHEIMER'S BLUE STORIES

Alzheimer's stories are both sad and humorous because it takes time for the disease to ravage the mind. Every family I visited had a story to tell about the disease. The first story is personal because my <u>mother performed</u> it one Sunday morning: I got up early and fed the dogs and placed mom's medicine into glass cups. She was taking seven tablets a day and one pill was cut in half. She was taking two and ½ pills at breakfast, two at lunch, and two and ½ at dinner. The procedure was difficult for mom because of her memory. Sunday morning anxiety kicked in and she looked more agitated than normal. I asked if she wanted to go to church. She said, "No, I am going to stay indoors today." She wanted to know if I was going fishing and I replied, "Yes, but I plan to leave at 11 a.m. and stay until 1 p.m. At that moment, I spilled some coffee on my red-hunting shirt. I thought about changing, but I was going fishing and it would likely get dirty anyway. After cooking mom's breakfast, I decided to put on a shirt like the one I was wearing, but blue in color. As I walked through the living room with the new shirt, mom asked, "Do you live here?" I said, "Yes, I take care of you." She asked, "Well, who are you?" I repeated, "I'm your son and I take care of you." She seemed happy at that answer, however, I cancelled the fishing trip for the day.

A <u>computer manager</u> remembered the following story about his grandma:Jim's grandma worked her entire career as a cook for a local school. After retiring, she was cooking a holiday meal and dropped the pinto beans on the floor. The beans were stored in quart jars and shattered with the beans. At lunch, grandma served the beans with glass pieces.

A <u>retired principal</u> remembered this story about the widow next door: He notice the widow next door was backing her car into the road and then pulling it back into the driveway. She kept pulling out and pulling in for an hour. Finally, he walked to her car and asked if she had car problems. She said, "No, I am just trying to get the man in the back seat out of my car."

A <u>retired salesman</u> remembered the following story about his wife: Bill's wife left to go to the grocery store at 9 a.m. He started to worry about her at 11 a.m. He called and she replied, "I don't know what town I am in, but it sure looks pretty." Police called him an hour later from a city over 100 miles away.

A <u>businessman</u> recalls the following story about his wife:

One morning I had just walked the dogs and my wife was on all fours on the front lawn. I asked, "Honey, what are you doing in our yard?" She replied, "These small sticks have to be picked up today. She had a handful of small sticks in her left hand.

The last story was <u>performed by mom</u> on the first day she was admitted to the Behavioral Hospital:

> Before admitted to the Behavioral Hospital, Intake Nurses pat patients down. They don't allow anything into the ward. After a pat down, my mother moved into her ward. The head nurse looked at me and asked if she had been checked for contraband. I said, "Yes!" The nurse was visibly upset as she worked her hands over mom's body. All of a sudden, the nurse pulled four pieces of cardboard, 6 inches by 10 inches long, from mom's midsection. I still laugh at the nurse asking, "Ms. Dollie, what is this?" My mother had every telephone number on four pieces of cardboard. She thought she would visit all week at the clinic. Phones aren't allowed on the ward. Patients are allowed to make calls during visiting hours. An angry nurse called the Intake Counselor and a big argument ensued over "cardboard."

CH. 26 STRANGERS DOING ALZHEIMER'S

Story 1

My fishing buddy told this true story concerning his two cousins who lived 100-yards away. They worked for the state over thirty-years. Etta and Ellen worked for the wildlife department in the licensing section. They were frugal all their lives. Both put money into an investment company for long-term growth. In forty years, Jon and Lucy watched them retire at age 65. This turned out to be a handy situation for Jon because they were close and he could take care of them. They had no living relatives other than Jon and Lucy, so it was natural for them to ask Jon and Lucy to be caregivers. And, it worked great until Etta and Ellen died twenty years later.

I got to know the cousins thru Jon when both women were in their late seventies. We all thought Ellen was getting Alzheimer's when I first met Jon and Lucy. Jon would tell funny stories about his transsexual cousin, Etta. Jon said he could tell they weren't aging at the same pace and Ellen being younger needed little help. We would be fishing and Jon would say, "I hate both of them!" I asked, "Why?" He said, "It has to do with a business deal we had many years ago." However, I could tell over the years and by the number of stories that Jon told, he really loved them! He was like a big brother to both of them. Jon and Lucy worked diligently to buy their medicine, food, and trips to the beauty shop. Jon and Lucy thought they were poor and did all they could to keep them above water. Jon did projects on their house and car for many years using his time and expertise.

Etta was the oldest of the two and both were in their eighties when these stories took root on Friday mornings. I fished on Friday morning with Jon for almost 20-years. During those years, Jon took Etta & Ellen fresh fish we caught. Both looked forward to the fish and a visit from Jon and Lucy. Etta told her neighbors, "Jon's fish-fillets were one of her favorite foods." They couldn't wait for Friday because they liked the fried fillets that Lucy cooked just for them using her special recipe!

Lucy would go to the grocery store on Friday while Jon and I fished. She bought all their food from a list the cousins made each week. Every Friday was the same routine for Jon and Lucy.

When the cousins became incapable of walking, Jon and Lucy had more to do and they enjoyed the time with their relatives. Lucy used the Bible in all of her views and the cousins enjoyed her thoughts and prayers. We added the cousins to our plans on Friday and it was always a good day for both families. Etta seemed to be the only one who didn't had dementia. Etta was the workhorse and kept everything running smoothly all those years.

Jon and Lucy noticed a strange thing occurring each week at Etta and Ellen's house. A strange truck would be in their driveway for several hours on a particular day. The truck became a regular attraction and curiosity. Finally Lucy asked Etta about the truck and who was visiting on Wednesdays. Etta replied, "Oh, that's Burt! He worked at the wildlife dept. with us for several years. He's working on our lawn and improving the flower beds around the house.

Jon and Lucy were in their late seventies and couldn't work in their flower beds, so they thought nothing about the extra help. However, this went on for over a year. Burt started moving things out of the house and Jon and Lucy began to worry. Both sisters died a year later. Burt had befriended both of them, fired their attorney, got Power of Attorney, and fired their doctor. He started a business helping the elderly. He developed "charge accounts" and ran up bills for landscape, bills for caregiver fees, travel, and business fees. The Will was changed so Burt could have 20% after the cousins died. Burt took over bank accounts and asked Jon and Lucy not to touch anything in the house.

This made Jon and Lucy upset because they were Etta and Ellen's only relatives. The final reading of the Will gave Burt $536,000 for his efforts. Rumors were rampant that Burt charged over $75K to their accounts before the will was read. This is a good example of a stranger doing Alzheimer's. The only thing the judge said about the situation was: "I sure wish a family member could have more say in the dispensation of their money. There are too many strangers in this will!"

Story 2

This true story is about two sons trying to work out the best way to take care of their mother with Alzheimer's. Eventually, one son takes over as the caregiver and isolates his brother. He got Power of Attorney and mentally removed his brother from his life. Yes, it can happen to caregivers and next of kin. I was close to this story for five years and documented the emotional battle in a notebook for months. The emotional story was good practice for caregivers on what not to do! Remember, we need relatives on our side to prevent fighting and confusion.

I fished with Jennie when I was going to college. We fished beautiful Tenkiller Lake almost every weekend. Her son would come by in his sail boat and say hello. Jennie had two sons that loved her. One son lived about forty miles away and often asked about the property and will.

Jennie was in a nursing home when the oldest son threw the will away. He excluded his brother from any further information about her health or the sale of her property. Jennie was a retired nurse that was in Stage-5 Alzheimer's at the age of 80. She got lost in her car and police called the family about her location. That incident was an indication she may need extra help. I was informed of the incident because I was close to both brothers. We worked on degrees in science and would get together at the cabin on weekends to sail and fish.

The oldest son got all property in his name once his dad died. He was caregiver for his mother and lived in her home after she was incapable of taking care of herself. She was moved to a nursing home at Stage 6 of the disease. Jennie's oldest son had a daughter to take care of and the strain was enormous on both sides of the family. Her oldest son was in his late-fifties and continued to work full-time. He had good caregiver skills, but needed to retire to do a great job for Jeannie.

Finally, Jennie's Will was discarded because the oldest son got Power of Attorney. The youngest son never got to read the will before it was thrown away. He never got a dime or any of his mother's property. The only excuse he ever heard was, "My mother and dad didn't want him to have any of the property—it was their wish!"

I always wanted to see the Will because I thought my fishing equipment might be mentioned. I left some expensive fishing equipment at their cabin one weekend. I never could recover the equipment from the brother. After all the property at the lake and in the city were sold, I knew my fishing poles were gone for good. The brother walked away with over $250,000. I am guessing the oldest son had some sort of problem sharing property with his younger brother. I never could get a handle on this "frightening story." I know many caregivers and they wouldn't wish these events on there loved one. But, it happens and some caregivers take control of grandma's property and never let go! Since his brother secretly took over all financial matters, no legal action was taken against him! Stories like these are common and caregivers must be on their "toes" to stop these "strangers." I have discovered it is common for family members not seek Power or Guardianship in dementia cases.

In my case, neighbors acted like "strangers" and took control of my position under the guise of wanting to help mother. The neighbor was a stranger doing Alzheimer's. If caregivers had more authority, Judy would have to ask for permission before she could make crazy decisions for our mother. Without my approval, she made a mess of the mom's care, property, and my ability to obtain Power or Guardianship in the future.

CH. 27 TOO YOUNG FOR ALZHEIMER'S?

According to the Alzheimer's Association, Alzheimer's is not just a disease of old age. Younger-onset (or early-onset) Alzheimer's disease affects people who are under the age of 65. Many people with younger-onset are in their 40s and 50s. They have families, careers, or are even caregivers themselves when Alzheimer's disease strikes. Up to 5 percent of people with Alzheimer's have younger-onset. In the U.S., that's almost 200,000 people. It's important to know you are not alone.[16] There are many ways to stay active and involved. Developing new hobbies is a good way. My friend bought a metal detector and his strength and stamina increased the first year. The disease affects each person differently and symptoms will vary.

Fishing, gardening, and walking are good alternatives to metal detecting. Remaining active is the primary goal. Walking is the best way to increase stamina and there are many walking trails around lakes, parks, and playgrounds.

If your finances will allow, going back to school is fun and exciting. I taught ten years at a university—mostly night classes. My biology classes were full of 40 to 60 year olds. They said they enjoyed getting back with the younger crowd and wanted to learn about the new theories of biology. They were auditing the class—they received no college credit, but they didn't care! I graded their papers and they just laughed at me for spending so much time on a non-credit student.

I remember one sixty-five-year-old man mention that he enjoyed my class because he could remain anonymous with the disease. He said, "I didn't want to hang out with old people at Senior Centers. Your class was perfect for people my age and no one knows I have Alzheimer's!"

Most people with younger-onset have the common type of Alzheimer's, which is not directly linked to genes. Doctors do not know why symptoms appear at unusually young age in these cases. In a few hundred families worldwide, scientists have found several rare genes that directly cause Alzheimer's. People who inherit these rare genes tend to develop symptoms in their 30s, 40s, and 50s.[17] Many people with Alzheimer's continue to live at home years into the disease. The caregivers have the time, money, and energy to manage the health for their partners or parents.

My mother moved from Stage one to Stage two in about a year. After her diagnosis, it is helpful to work with family members to prepare for changes coming in the household. I was living with Mom but her two daughters lived more than nine hours away.

I volunteered to be mom's caregiver and wrote letters and e-mails to her daughters stating my intentions. I wanted to make sure everyone understood that I would be her caregiver. My qualifications made me a good choice to take the caregiver job.

If you live in a suburb, make sure everyone knows it is dementia and you are going to help her/him live at home as long as possible. Any caregiver changes can be made if the family votes to change. It is vital that you contact everyone by e-mail, on a regular basis, even if nothing changes. The first e-mail should inform friends and relatives that someone has been selected to make all the decisions. The friends and relatives that don't have e-mail, should provide an address and phone number for contact. You should ask for suggestions, but remember, the family has agreed on a primary caregiver. CASE CLOSE!!

CH. 28 HELPING FAMILY AND FRIENDS COPE

Your spouse or partner may feel a sense of loss or loneliness as a result of the changes the diagnosis brings. What you can do to help your spouse or partner:

- Continue to take part in all the activities that you can. Adapt activities to fit what you are comfortable with and enjoy.
- Find new activities that you can do together. Sometimes befriending another couple in the same situation offers new possibilities for support.
- Talk with your spouse or partner about how he or she can assist you—and what you can still do on your own.
- Work with your spouse or partner to put together a file with information you may need later about caregiver services and their costs, including housekeeping and respite (caregiver relief) care.
- Continue to find ways for you and your spouse or partner to fulfill the need for intimacy.
- Encourage your spouse or partner to attend a support group and Stay connected with family and friends.[18]

Children often experience a wide range of emotions. Younger children may be afraid that they will get the disease or that they did something to cause it.

Teenagers may become resentful when they have to take on more responsibilities for helping around the home. Or, they may feel embarrassed that their parent is "different." College-bound children may be reluctant to leave home to attend school.

The Alzheimer's Association recommends the following to help your children:

1) Talk openly about the changes you are expecting because of the disease.
2) Find out what their emotional needs are. Find ways to support them, like meeting with a counselor who specializes in children who have a loved one with Alzheimer's.
3) Notify school social workers and teachers about your situation. Give them information about the disease.
4)
   Invite children to attend support group meetings. Include them in counseling sessions.
   Don't pull away. Try to find activities together you can still enjoy together. If you can't drive, plan a hike or bike ride. Check out public transportation in your area.
5) Make it okay to laugh. Sometimes humor lightens the mood and makes coping easier.
6) Record your thoughts, feelings, and wisdom in writing, audio or video. Your children will appreciate this when they grow older.[19]

Friends, co-workers, and neighbors may not understand what is happening to you. Neighbors told ADULT SERVICES mom was scared of me and that's why she wandered. This previous sentence is a complete lie.

It is common for a person with dementia to wander and become lost; many do repeatedly. Wandering can be dangerous—even life threatening.[20]

The Alzheimer's Association recommends the following ways to help your friends:

1) Share your experiences of living with Alzheimer's disease.
2) Invite them to Alzheimer's Association education programs and events.
3) Continue social activities as much as possible. Seek out local programs specifically for people with dementia.
4) Let your friends know what you are still comfortable doing
5) Let them know when you need help and support—and tell them what they can do.[21]

My mother and I got together and read her will and discussed where she wanted to live. She said, "I want to live in my house until I die!" I told her I would do my best. If your health deteriorates, "What do you want me to do?" She said, "Sell the house and put me into a nursing home!" I said, "Okay, I will tell my sisters your wishes and that's what we will do.

I didn't know Mom would start wandering and tell everybody she was in danger at home. She told everybody she was scared of teens in the front yard and scared of a man that looks into her windows at night who lives in the shed behind the house. I didn't know all these were symptoms of "suspicion behavior" and it would wreck her present lifestyle! We had no idea a nurse and a police officer would wreck all of her wishes.

Yes, things can change! Prepare for these changes and be ready for them. What changes will you have to make if your loved one wanders? What will you do? Legally appoint a person you trust to make financial and health care decisions on your behalf when you cannot. Tell the person your wishes for the future, including where you want to live and what typ of treatments you want or don't want. Always plan ahead for possible changes in your loved one.

My grandpa lived to ninety-seven with Alzheimer's. I believed he lived that long because he never used alcohol, tobacco, or drugs. I worked with him every summer and was with him breakfast, lunch and dinner. He always ate small portions and had a simple diet; He never carried bags of cooked beans from Mexico or green tea from Japan. I don't believe he ever took a bite of dark chocolate in his life. In the fifties and sixties, adults didn't consume candy or sweets like we do today.

Doctors recommend that we "Eat a variety of foods." Grandpa worked hard and got plenty of exercise climbing ladders and crawling into attics. I know because he had me following with his bag of tools.

As a kid, I often asked for a hamburger and fries for lunch. Grandpa always said, "No!" This was the late fifties, and hamburger meat wasn't kept cold in some restaurants to diminish the bacteria. It was common to hear someone dying after eating a hamburger. He said, "Your having a steak with me; They're safe to eat." Years later, we wondered if dementia had something to do when he discouraged me eating hamburgers. You can probably guess my reaction to lunch. I complained all the time about steaks and stopped eating them at age 12. I rarely eat steaks except on special occasions.

Two of the most important ways you can take good care of yourself are to stay healthy and safe. What caregivers can do about your health:

1) Get regular check-ups.
2) Exercise regularly, with your doctor's approval.
3) Rest when you are tired.
4) Adopt a healthy diet.
5) Take any prescribed medications as directed.
6) Cut down on alcohol—it can worsen symptoms.
7) Ask for help when you need it.
8) Reduce stress in your life, and learn new ways to relax.
9) Stay socially engaged.[22]

Symptoms of Alzheimer's, like loss of memory and decision-making ability, can bring about new safety needs. What can you do about your safety:

a) Keep important phone numbers nearby.

b) Post reminders to lock doors and turn off electrical appliances.

Arrange for an in-home helper to assist you when your spouse, partner, or caregiver needs to be away from home.

Arrange for other ways to get around when it is no longer safe for you to drive.

c) Enroll in MedicAlert ®+ Alzheimer's Association Safe Return® for services to assist you, should you ever become lost.

Purchase the Alzheimer's Association Comfort Zone®, a new web-based GPS location management service that can help families achieve some peace of mind. Comfort Zone uses the Internet and a small device to ensure that you and your family are always connected.[23]

CH. 29 COURT CASE

I went to court and mother was present. By the time the hearing started about ten days from the issue of the PO, I knew that the Deputy hadn't told the Heart Hospital mother had dementia. Also, He hadn't told CARE, INC. about her dementia because the city police reported to me they didn't know about mother's dementia and wandering. I knew there was a conspiracy related to my previous complaints of an Officer lying in a report during my divorce. But, I decided to leave the conspiracy theory alone for fear of sounding stupid at the hearing. There would be plenty of time to ask the FBI and Justice Department to check it out!

The Adult Care, Inc. people who was taking care of her, had asked her p-c doctor to take mom off all medications except for thyroid medication and eye drops. I looked at the elderly judge and he acted as if "his memory" could be lacking. I tried to trick him and believe it or not, I was successful. I wasn't allowed to contact the doctor to ask him why he took mother off the medication we worked so hard getting her to take. The protective order (PO) wouldn't allow contacting any of the people during the three months. However, I did have enough time to file complaints on everybody during those three months, including a judge for lying and civil rights violations. Remember, the first judge okayed a PO without question from ADULT CARE, INC.

Right off the bat, I caught the judge lying about mom's medication. I knew it was time to listen carefully because my attorney directed me to give the judge the "diagnosis sheet" and that would be enough to exonerate me from the PO. She was sure the judge couldn't continue the hearing with the sheet showing mom had "dementia."

ADULT CARE, INC. stated, under oath, they had asked mom's p-c doctor to remove all meds and he did. Mom's med sheet should have just one medication other than her eye drops. However, the judge wasn't listening to the testimony and ask to see all medication sheets. I told him my sheet has six medications not including her eye drops. "My list was up-to-date,"

I reminded the judge. I said, "Your honor, I hope their list has six drugs on it! I was betting the judge had already forgotten what was said in his court minutes before. After a few minutes the judge nodded, "Both sheets have the same drugs!" I almost called the judge a liar in court, but didn't because that lying would be used at the Council as a repeat complaint. I shook my head to show my disrespect for the judge. I couldn't believe I caught the elderly judge lying in court for ADULT CARE, INC.

Then the judge asked me why I didn't give the Deputy mom's medication when the Deputy came by at 8 p.m.

I told the judge the officer wanted all of her medicine and I only had four of the six on hand. I had two ordered at Wal-Mart but they wouldn't be ready for pickup until tomorrow morning.

The next day I drove to the State Capitol to file on the judge for lying. All States have a Council for citizens to complain about judges. After reviewing my complaint of lying, the Council turned down my first complaint. The complaint list for removing a judge has some thirty reasons or "causes" for the judge to be removed from the bench.

However, I signed a petition on a Web Site asking the judge to remove himself from the bench for a list of previous-bad rulings. Perhaps, attrition would cause the judge to be dismissed or even retire. I often wondered if the elderly judge had dementia or Alzheimer's.

My six-drug sheet was important because the Deputy told the ER staff at the hospital that I didn't give mom's drugs to him or the ambulance driver. I still believe the officer's statement was some sort of retribution that only an officer with mental problems could contrive. I regret the e- mail to this Deputy because his behavior made me cautious when he arrived to look for mom when she wandered.

I caught the officer lying because I gave the ambulance driver this same six-drug list three nights before. The officer wasn't present when the ambulance picked up mom on Monday or Thursday afternoon. This six- drug list was handed to the driver the previous Monday night when she was taken to the ER at her Behavioral Hospital. I could see the list on her chest after she was placed on the gurney on both nights. They evidently place drug lists on the patient after they strap them to the gurney.

As I have stated in this book, caregivers have to be on their toes with judges and police officers. They know nothing about dementia or Alzheimer's. The Deputy didn't attend court and I wondered why because he was the one who forced legal action against me! They are "Strangers" because they don't know the disease like we do! The ordeal cost me $1,200 for motels for the ten days. I spent the six months writing this book and filing complaints. This book documents actions by so-called experts in dementia and Alzheimer's. These state organizations attack caregivers because we know our "stuff" and they "don't!"

Caregivers that witness lying must file soon after you see it in court. It is your civic duty! The same standard holds true for police officers. We can't maintain a good legal system if everybody keeps their mouth shut! Judges and police officers aren't trained in Alzheimer's—they get some training in mental health but it comes down to the officers' ability to make a good decision about the individual who has the disease!

TIP: Always ask an attorney to go to court with you if a PO occurs in your career. They can answer questions in Alzheimer's cases. I wanted a trial for my PO and no jury would accuse me of abuse after hearing all the facts! The three-month extension of the PO was a shotgun approach used to mistreat caregivers.

My mother told the judge that she needed a bottle of eye drops. Mom asked DD, the advocate who wrote the PO for mom, to take her home and she would get it from her nightstand. She told the judge I have a full bottle of eye drops on my bedroom table. Then she paused for a moment and said,

"She didn't want to use that bottle because J.P. probably poisoned it while she was gone." I briefly glanced at the judge to see if he were awake to hear a textbook-version of an Alzheimer's statement. Mom was talking in Alzheimer's language and it was coming, as they say, from "the horse's mouth!" The judge said nothing! The judge's secretary shook her head in disgust.

This statement proved mom was still paranoid ten days later. I watched and listened to the judge for a short time and guessed it passed him rather quickly. I believe, and no one can change my mind, the judge did all he could to save ADULT CARE, INC. from embarrassment by lying for them. I don't know why a judge would want to save a dishonest business! I told only a few stories to educate everybody in court. I knew, by this time, I was likely the most knowledgeable person about the disease in the courtroom. I had a rowdy class of students to teach complex symptoms of Alzheimer's disease. That is when I decided to write this book and help educate the public about this crazy disease and the people who "PLAY" with it I filed on the court judge twice: once for lying about the medications and another for showing favoritism to ADULT CARE, INC. I filed on the first judge for violating my civil rights by signing a PO without proof of abuse.

I thought mom could live another four or five years in her home and wanted the psychiatric hospital's opinion. I thought she was in Stage-four of the disease and considered myself an expert in the disease. Why couldn't mom live at home for another five years? The hospital agreed and offered their expertise when I needed help with mother. The Behavioral Hospital was open 24/7 for caregivers needing emergency help. TIP: Place the phone number of the Intake Coordinator on that yellow-legal pad containing telephone numbers.

Your mother/dad can live a long and productive life at home with help from these unsung HEROS. My grandpa lived a long life because he had a younger wife that could handle all of his needs with the disease. Margo worked with grandpa when no one knew what Alzheimer's meant. They were a good team from the start. She was a great caregiver and I was glad the two of them worked so well together. Her skill and patience helped him live a long time.

But, as you probably know, the judge was slow and ruled that the PO would be extended another three months. I added these three months to my third complaint: lying about meds, showing favoritism to Adult Care, Inc., and extending a PO without proof or reason.

This court appearance was a sham and minutes were not recorded! The elderly judge didn't know why my mother behaved the way she did—mom has been in Stage 3 Alzheimer's for the past year.

I never had a chance to tell the judge that mom's dad died from the disease. I did ask the judge, "Please don't lecture me about this disease,

Your Honor!" After the extension of the PO, I wasn't in any mood to listen to people discussing the disease who didn't know anything about dementia or Alzheimer's.

Finally I said, "Your Honor, my mother needed at least four-more weeks in the Behavioral Hospital to function at a normal level for her age and condition. Since she didn't get that treatment, she has problems communicating with her three kids when they visit, she has made some bad decisions, she is often anxious, and her mood and personality have changed drastically.

I blame the people in this book for not having the courage and training to make good choices dealing with this fatal disease. Your Honor, Strangers shouldn't be doing Alzheimer's!"

BIBLIOGRAPHY

1   Alzheimer's Association, "basics of Alzheimer's disease, What it is and What can you do 800-272-3900, 2014: pamphlet #770-10-0003. p. 1.

2   Alzheimer's Association, "behaviors," How to respond when dementia causes unpredictable behaviors, 800-272-3900, 2014: pamphlet #77010-0021. p. 8.

3   Alzheimer's Association, "basics of Alzheimer's disease, What it is and What can you do 800-272-3900, 2014: pamphlet #770-10-0003. p. 10.

4   Alzheimer's Association, "behaviors," How to respond when dementia causes unpredictable behaviors, 800-272-3900, 2014: pamphlet # 770-10-0021. p. 9.

5   Ibid., p 8.

6   Alzheimer's Association, "basics of Alzheimer's disease," What it is and What can you do 800-272-3900, 2014: pamphlet # 770-10-0003. p. 1.

7   Ibid., p 10.

8   Ibid., p 8.

9   Ibid., p 10-11.

10   Ibid., p 3.

11   Ibid., p 18.

12   Ibid., p 14-17.

13   Ibid., p 3.

14   Alzheimer's Association, "behaviors", How to respond when dementia causes unpredictable behaviors 800-272-3900, 2014: pamphlet #770-10-0021. p. 8.

15   Ibid., p 3.

16   Alzheimer's Association, "younger-onset Alzheimer's," I'm too young to have Alzheimer's disease. 800-272-3900, 2011: pamphlet # 773-10-0004. p. 1.

17   Ibid., p 1.

18   Ibid., p 3.

19   Ibid., p 4.

20   Alzheimer's Association, "Six out of 10 people with Alzheimer's will wander," You can't know when it will happen, but you'll know what to do when it does. 800-272-3900, 2012: card #775-20-0002. p 1.

21   Alzheimer's Association, "younger-onset Alzheimer's, I'm too young to have Alzheimer's disease. 800-272-3900, 2011: pamphlet # 773-10-0004. p. 5.

22   Ibid., p. 9.

23   Ibid., p. 9.

SPECIAL NOTE

Permission granted for cover picture of mom on her fifth birthday in 1935. The picture was taken on the front porch of their log cabin in Kenwood, Oklahoma. Permission to print "MY VISIT WITH JESUS in summary format given by mother in 2010.

I would like to thank the Alzheimer's Association (alz.org) for their help with my book. This disease is going to take a lot of time and money to defeat. This book is not associated with the Alzheimer's Association or any other organization with a similar name.

AUTHOR BIOGRAPHY

I was born in Pryor, OK. My dad was a sharecropper and my mother owned three grocery stores in the Salina, Kenwood, and Chouteau area. I was reared in Oaks, OK and lived on a strawberry and dairy farm.

I taught in the public schools in Oklahoma and Missouri for twenty-seven years. I taught at the college level for ten years. I invented three chemistry toys that are used by schools throughout the U.S. in science classes. I taught caregiver education at Ft. Riley, Kansas for the Army-Medical Corps.

DEDICATION

I would like to dedicate this book to my three kids: Aaron, Joel, and Eleanor. I would like to add Esther to my dedication because all four suffered during the year I worked on the book. All four missed months of allowance without questioning my reason. I did mention something about my book educating young people throughout the country about a deadly disease. I believed when I mentioned "terrifying disease" and "young people" in the same sentence, it caused them to come on board and sacrifice a few luxuries.

CPSIA information can be obtained
at www.ICGtesting.com
Printed in the USA
FSOW02n0740010316
17377FS